VOLLEYBALL

VOLLEYBALL

Steven Boga

STACKPOLE
BOOKS

Published by
STACKPOLE BOOKS
5067 Ritter Road
Mechanicsburg, PA 17055

Printed in United States of America

10 9 8 7 6 5 4 3 2 1

First edition

Cover design by Caroline Miller with Wendy Baugher

Library of Congress Cataloging-in-Publication Data

Boga, Steve, 1947–
        Volleyball / by Steve Boga.—1st ed.
            p. cm.
        ISBN 0-8117-2491-3 (alk. paper)
        1. Volleyball. I. Title.
    GV1015.3.B65   1997
    796.325—dc20   96-21976
                                                                            CIP

CONTENTS

Introduction vii

History 1

Court and Equipment 5

Technique 13

Strategy 53

Winning the Mental Game 59

Getting Better 65

Rules 77

Glossary 91

Resources 97

INTRODUCTION

···

Don't let what you cannot do interfere
with what you can do.
　　　　　　　　　　—John Wooden

I was in Athens the first time I ever saw elite volleyball. Rumania played Bulgaria in the first match; Turkey versus Greece in the second. The standing-room-only crowd was in a frenzy from start to finish, their passions fueled by nationalistic fervor and oceans of ouzo and retsina. On the court, little guys were diving and setting, big guys leaping and spiking. It was an exhibition of acrobatics not seen since the circus was in town.

A week later on the island of Crete, I played in a pick-up volleyball game with about twenty players to a side. The first time I rotated to left-front, I found myself staring across the net at a seventy-year-old woman wearing a Davy Crockett coonskin cap; a short time later, I squared off with an eight-year-old boy. The contrast between this match and the ones in Athens was stark and unavoidable. At the same time, I was struck by the game's capacity for diversity; volleyball has room for seventy-year-old women in coonskin caps and eight-year-old boys, as well as diving Greeks and spiking Turks.

It is in fact a very versatile, flexible game. You can play indoors or out, in gyms or at the beach, anything goes or by the book, pitty-pat or set-and-smash.

This book is for those who want to rise above pitty-pat and enter the exhilarating world of set-and-smash. Welcome.

In the pages that follow, you will learn about volleyball technique, strategy, and rules. Before you can make sense of those, however, you must have a basic understanding of how the game is played, including vocabulary. Pay particular attention to the italicized buzzwords in the following primer. More detailed explanations follow in the text and in the glossary at the back of the book.

A *match* begins with a coin toss between the two team captains. The captain who wins the toss may select the playing side or choose to serve first, the other captain receiving the remaining choice. The right to first serve alternates with each game until the deciding (third or fifth) game of the match, when a second toss is made. Teams change sides at eight points of the deciding game, unless both captains agree at the time of the coin toss not to switch.

Indoor volleyball is usually six against six, and competitive beach volleyball is usually two against two. But unofficial games can accommodate just about any number of players.

If the match is officiated, the referee gives a signal and the player in the right-back position (from the point of view of the serving team) has five seconds to initiate the serve from behind the baseline. The server must use one hand or arm to make contact. The ball must travel over the legal portion of the net—that is, between the *antennae*—and may not touch the net. If the server makes a bad toss, she may let the ball drop to the floor untouched and begin again, with an additional five seconds for the second attempt. The server may not step on or over the baseline until after the ball is contacted.

During play:

- The ball must pass over the legal portion of the net—that is, between the antennae.
- A ball landing on a boundary line is in.
- A player may go off the court to play a ball.
- A ball coming from the opponent that is perceived to be *out-of-bounds* may not be caught until it legally touches an out-of-bounds area.
- The ball may contact any number of body parts as long as it does so more or less simultaneously.
- Each team is allowed a maximum of three consecutive contacts before the ball must be returned to the

opponents' side of the court. If the first touch is a *block*, the team still gets three more contacts.

- Except on the serve, the ball is in play if it touches the legal part of the net.

wrong ➤

- A player may not touch the net while the ball is in play, though such touches having nothing to do with the play will be ignored.
- No *net fault* occurs when the ball is driven into the net with such force that it contacts an opponent.
- On the *follow-through* after a *spike*, the hands may legally pass over the net.
- The feet are the only part of the body that may touch the opponents' court, and, even then, part of the foot must be on or above the *centerline* at the time of contact.
- Once the ball is *dead,* it is not a fault to hit the net or cross over the centerline. A ball is dead when it touches the playing surface, when it is ruled out-of-bounds, or when a *rally* ends due to a referee's whistle.
- A player may not spike the ball until part of the ball is on his side of the net.
- It is a *held-ball fault* when the ball comes to rest, even momentarily, in the hands or on the arms of a player.
- It is a *double-contact fault* when one player contacts the ball two times in a row—that is, without another player's contacting it in between those two hits. Exception: a blocker who contacts the ball may, without penalty, be the first to contact it after the block.
- If the ball is held simultaneously by two opposing players, it is a *double-fault* and the point should be played over. It should be played over any time two opponents commit simultaneous faults.
- If two players on the same team simultaneously touch the ball, it is considered two touches for that team.
- Blockers may reach over the net and block the ball if the ball would have cleared the net had it been untouched by a defending player.
- If two teammates contact the ball on a block, it is counted as only one hit.

- In indoor six-person volleyball, only front-row players may block. Back-row players may not block and may spike only when they take off (jump) from behind the attack line.

• • • • •

Thanks to the setters and spikers everywhere who gave me inspiration. Special thanks to USA Volleyball for its support and to John Kessel, director of program development, for his encouragement and generous editorial help.

HISTORY

In 1895 William Morgan, a YMCA instructor in Holyoke, Massachusetts, invented a game he called *mintonette*. By blending elements of basketball, baseball, handball, and tennis, Morgan created a sport for his classes of local businessmen who found basketball too rough-and-tumble. He borrowed the net from tennis and raised it so the top was 6 feet 6 inches above the floor, only slightly higher than the average man's head.

During a demonstration game, a man named J. Halsted remarked that the players seemed to be *volleying* the ball back and forth over the net, and suggested that perhaps *volleyball* would be a more descriptive name for the sport. On July 7, 1896, Springfield College in Massachusetts was the site of the first volleyball game.

Volleyball spread like a brushfire, its popularity due in part to its simplicity—few rules, few players, few basic skills, minimal equipment—and its adaptability. Players of disparate fitness levels could play on surfaces from hardwood to sand.

After World War II, volleyball became more strategic, with detailed offensive and defensive schemes. Years before, the Filipinos had added the set-and-spike to the game, and the Japanese now built on that to create a style of play called power volleyball. It required players to dive and roll to recover shots and to jump high to spike and serve. Men's and women's teams from Japan, the Soviet Union, and East Germany used this style to dominate international competition through the seventies.

Although volleyball was invented in the United States, it wasn't until the mideighties that America began to play a leading role on the international stage. No doubt its clout was intensified by its rather sudden emergence as a volleyball powerhouse. In 1984, for the first time ever, both the U.S. men's and women's

Highlights of the Volley Ball Rules, taken from the 1897 Association Athletic League Handbook:

III. Court. The exact size of the court may change to suit the convenience of the place.

IV. Net. The top line of the net must be six feet six inches from the floor.

V. Ball. The ball shall be a rubber bladder covered with leather or canvas.

VI. Server and Service. The server shall stand with one foot on the back line. The ball must be batted with the hand. Two services or trials are allowed him to place the ball in the opponents' court (as in tennis). In a service, the ball must be batted at least ten feet, no dribbling allowed. To dribble the ball is to carry it all the time, keeping it bouncing. When dribbling the ball no player shall cross the dribbling line, this putting the ball out of play and counting against him.

A service which would strike the net, but which is struck by another of the same side before striking the net, if it goes over into the opponents' court, is good, but if it should go outside, the server has no second trial.

VIII. Net Ball. A play which hits the net, aside from first service, is called a net ball, and is equivalent to a failure to return, counting for the opposite side. The ball hitting the net on first service shall be called dead, and counts as a trial.

IX. Line Ball. It is a ball striking the boundary line. It is equivalent to one out of court, and counts as such.

X. Play and Players. Any number may play that is convenient to the place. A player should be able to cover about ten by ten feet.

Helps in Playing the Game

Strike the ball with both hands.

Look for uncovered space in the opponents' field.

Play together; cover your own space.

Pass from one to another when possible.

Watch the play constantly, especially the opponents'.

teams won Olympic medals. The men defeated Brazil to capture the gold, while the women lost to China in the finals, taking home the silver. The U.S. men won the gold again at the 1988 Olympics, both teams took bronze medals in 1992, and of this writing both teams are ranked in the top five in the world.

Volleyball continues to attract a wide range of participants, from young to old, hacker to elite. At the top, power volleyball is fast and exciting, with acrobatic leaps and dives, and spikes up to seventy miles per hour. At the recreation level, the sport is ideal for city leagues, as well as at picnics and family gatherings. It is one of the few sports that can be enjoyed coed.

> **The Japanese added volleyball to the Olympic Games program in 1964, causing a growth spurt in both popularity and proficiency that continues today.**

The appeal of volleyball transcends cultural barriers; its worldwide popularity is second only to soccer and comparable to basketball. The International Volleyball Federation estimates that 800 million people—46 million of them in the United States—play the game at least occasionally in 210 countries.

If you're thinking of adding yourself to that list, it's never too late to get involved. For volleyball is truly a lifetime sport.

VOLLEYBALL TIME LINE

1895   Volleyball invented by William Morgan.

1896   Morgan's handwritten copy of volleyball rules turned over to the YMCA Physical Director's Conference.

1897   Official volleyball rules included in Handbook of the Athletic League of YMCAs of North America.

1900   Special ball designed for the sport.

1916   Spalding Blue Cover volleyball rule book published; National Collegiate Athletic Association (NCAA) invited to join with YMCA to promote the game.

1916   In the Philippines, the set-and-spike introduced.

1917   Game changed from twenty-one to fifteen points.

1920   Three hits per side and back-row attack rules instituted.

1922   In Brooklyn, first YMCA national championships, with twenty-seven teams from eleven states represented.

1928   United States Volleyball Association (USVBA) formed; first U.S. Open staged, with the field open to non-YMCA members.

1930   First two-man beach game played.

1934   National volleyball referees recognized and approved.

1937   At the Amateur Athletic Union (AAU) convention in Boston, USVBA recognized as the official national governing body of the sport in the United States.

1946   Avery Brundage invited to advise USVBA on steps required for recognition of volleyball as an Olympic sport.

1947   The Federation Internationale de Volley-Ball (FIVB) founded in Paris; USVBA a charter member.

1948   In California, first official two-person beach tournament held.

1948   U.S. Volleyball Team made a goodwill trip to Europe.

1949   First world championships held in Prague, Czechoslovakia.

1954   Volleyball Hall of Fame established in Los Angeles.

1955   Volleyball included in Pan American Games at Mexico City.

1958   Official score sheet created.

1964   Volleyball introduced to the Olympic Games in Tokyo.

1974   World championships in Mexico telecast in Japan.

1974   In San Diego, first beach tournament with prize money held.

1975   U.S. national women's team began year-round training regime.

1977   U.S. national men's team began year-round training regime.

1983   The Association of Volleyball Professionals (AVP) formed.

1984   The United States won its first volleyball medals at the Olympics in Los Angeles; the men took the gold, the women the silver.

1986   The Women's Professional Volleyball Association (WPVA) formed.

1988   U.S. men captured the Olympic gold medal in Korea.

1988   Cash prizes awarded in twenty-eight beach tournaments.

1990   World League created.

1992   United States won double bronze medals in Barcelona Olympics.

1994   Total prize money for beach events reached $4 million.

1995   Volleyball celebrated its 100th anniversary.

1996   Two-person beach volleyball added to the Olympic Games in Atlanta, with twenty-four men's teams and sixteen women's teams competing. U.S. men's teams won both the gold and the silver.

COURT AND EQUIPMENT

$\cdots\cdots\cdots\cdots\cdots\cdots\cdots\cdots\cdots\cdots\cdots\cdots\cdots$

Volleyball is refreshingly low-tech. All you really need is a ball and a net. No net? Just tie string or rope between two objects. No set boundaries or yardstick? Just step off a court and throw down some shirts and towels for markers.

COURT

Although an official volleyball court (fig 1) is 29 feet 6 inches (9 meters) wide and 59 feet (18 meters) long (29.5 feet per side), don't feel you have to stand on ceremony. The backyard game can be played on a court of almost any size and shape. It will certainly shrink or stretch to accommodate an ill-placed stump or rhododendron.

Avoid rough, wet, or slippery terrain, especially if it looks dangerous. Try to make the court horizontal, its surface smooth and consistent. Sand offers a hospitable playing surface for those who like to throw their bodies around.

To build a sand court away from the beach, dig out an area 59 feet by 29.5 feet, plus at least a 6.5-foot border all the way around (10 feet would be better), to a depth of about 12 inches, and fill it with sand. The best sand for a court is the finest grained available. Lay down rope for boundaries; rope will jump when struck by the ball, making it easy to settle boundary disputes. To each corner of the rope, tie a 3-foot piece of rope with a scrap of wood attached to the other end. Bury the wood in the sand to ensure that the rope boundary is not pulled out of line during play.

No matter what court size you use, try to maintain a "free zone" of at least 6 feet 6 inches (2 meters) around the court's perimeter. An indoor court should have an obstruction-free area of at least 23 feet (7 meters) above the playing surface. In major

Figure 1. Basic court diagram with dimensions.

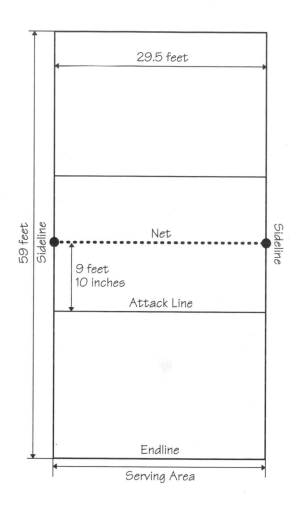

29.5 feet

59 feet

Sideline

Sideline

Net

9 feet
10 inches

Attack Line

Endline

Serving Area

competitions, the free zone extends at least 19 feet (6 meters) out from the sidelines, 29 feet (9 meters) from the baselines, and 40 feet (12.5 meters) above the playing surface.

Indoor courts should be of one color, preferably light and bright, with the free zone of a contrasting color (a requirement in major international competition).

The court lines, officially 2 inches (5 centimeters) wide, form part of the 59-foot by 29.5-foot playing area. A *centerline,* a marked or unmarked line directly beneath the net, divides the court into two equal halves. On each side of the court, a line is drawn parallel to, and 9.5 feet (3 meters) from, the centerline. These are called the *attack lines;* the area between them and the centerline is called the *front court,* and the area between the attack lines and the baselines is called the *backcourt.* It's important to include attack lines, because backcourt players may not spike in the frontcourt.

NET

Look for an all-weather mesh net with sleeves and reinforcing tape on the top, bottom, and sides. Look for easy setup that doesn't require digging holes. Park and Son (formerly Forster Manufacturing Company) makes volleyball sets for beginners and intermediates that include a 30-foot by 3-foot sleeved net with 4-inch mesh and colorful top, bottom, and side tapes. It can be firmly stretched between two no-rust PVC posts. The best models include posts with push-button adjustments, allowing you to set the height to official men's, women's, and coed levels.

If you want to construct a semi-permanent court in your yard, you will achieve maximum stability if you set both net poles in five-gallon, concrete-filled cans, and bury them.

Many companies carry adjustable-sleeved nets that can be used in 30-, 22-, and 15-foot lengths by simply relocating the sleeve. This feature can be handy if you have limited space or fewer than six players on a side.

The typical net anchoring system consists of guy ropes, tension clips, and four high-visibility polypropylene ground stakes. For sand play, however, some sets have plastic beach disks, essentially Frisbees with holes in the center. The guy lines attach to the disks, which are buried in the sand. This keeps them in place and guarantees maximum net tension. Alternatively, the disks can be used to secure the boundaries.

Whether you use a topflight, durable mesh net or just a rope strung between two trees, keep the net taut and at the proper height. Allowing the net to sag much below 8 feet in height is an invitation for the game to deteriorate into jungle ball.

BALL

If you play volleyball even semiregularly, you should spend the money for a good-quality leather ball. Unless you are forced to play on rough concrete, stay away from rubber playground balls. Leather costs more than rubber, but it's worth the expense. The extreme bounciness of rubber balls makes it impossible to get the good touch needed for precise passes and sets. Moreover, rubber balls can sting the arms, which probably explains why so many beginners swat at the ball instead of executing a proper forearm pass.

The ball should have a round, flexible leather (or synthetic leather) cover over a rubber (or similar) bladder. The circumference is 25.5–26 inches (65–67 centimeters), the weight 10–10.5 ounces (260–280 grams).

The February 1995 issue of *Volleyball* magazine reviewed sixty-five different volleyballs. The best were tagged "Editor's Choice." Five others were rated "Best Value," meaning they are high-quality balls at an affordable price.

Beach Balls over $50

Spalding AVP Top-Flite 18	$80.00	Editor's Choice
Brine BV10WP WPVA Pro Tour	$68.00	Editor's Choice
Brine Hard Core Pro	$64.00	Editor's Choice
Brine BV13WP Pro Circuit	$54.00	* Best Value

Beach Balls from $21–$49.99

Mikasa VSSA	$40.00	Editor's Choice
Brine BVC40 Beach Club	$31.00	Editor's Choice
Molten Bandana Beach	$30.00	Editor's Choice
Brine BV80WP Surf & Turf	$22.00	* Best Value

Beach Balls under $20.99

Molten Summer Sand	$18.00	Editor's Choice
Regent Beachtime	$14.99	* Best Value

Indoor Balls over $49

Mikasa VFC200	$70.00	Editor's Choice
Molten IV58L Super Touch	$55.00	Editor's Choice
Tachikara SV5W	$54.95	* Best Value

Indoor Balls under $49

Wilson Soft Touch	$39.95	Editor's Choice
Mikasa VFC210	$38.00	Editor's Choice
Tachikara SV5WS	$34.95	Editor's Choice
Tachikara SV18S	$27.95	* Best Value

A good leather ball will last at least a couple of years of indoor play. Playing on sand will shorten its life somewhat, though not nearly as much as playing on asphalt or concrete. The playground will beat up your leather ball in no time.

Balls can become egg-shaped, so it's nice to know that all companies replace defective balls; however, don't abuse this guarantee. If your ball was run over by a car or chewed by a dog, it's not the company's fault, and you may end up without even an egg-shaped ball.

To keep a ball from egging:
- Never leave it for a long time in an exceedingly hot or cold environment, such as a car trunk in the summer.
- Don't use it as a pillow or seat.
- When not in use, overinflate it until it is hard. Let the excess air out when you play and reinflate it after you're done.

The best conditioning program for a new volleyball is simply to put it in play. It will be stiff at first, but as it gets older, it develops a better feel. As beach volleyballs age, they absorb sweat and suntan lotion and get heavier. But that can be an advantage in erratic outdoor winds, so beach tournaments generally use balls at least a few months old.

SHOES

Sand players can go barefoot, but everyone else should wear shoes with adequate support and grip. Stay away from running shoes, which lack the support necessary for lateral movement. Look for athletic shoes with enough cushioning to withstand the pounding the feet take when jumping to block and spike. High-tops weigh a little more but offer greater ankle support.

Playing barefoot on grass is a sensous pleasure, but you have better traction with shoes. Even low-top athletic shoes offer some protection against sprained ankles.

If you do wear shoes, you should wear socks. Otherwise, your feet will sweat and slide around inside your shoes. If you plan to play several games in one day, you may want extra socks. And if the sand is too hot for bare feet, you may decide to play in socks and no shoes.

Here are the toll-free phone numbers for the major volleyball shoe companies:

Asics:	800/678-9435
Kaepa:	800/880-9200
Mizuno:	800/966-1234
New Balance:	800/343-4648
Nike:	800/344-6453
Power:	800/437-2526
Reebok:	800/843-4444

CLOTHING

It's hard to find a sport with a looser dress code than volleyball. Comfort and freedom of movement are key, and so shorts and cotton T-shirts are popular. If you're on a recreation team, you will probably wear a uniform, usually nothing more than a T-shirt that matches your teammates'. If you play at the beach in fine weather, you will probably wear very little: shorts and T-shirt, tank top, or bare chest for men; shorts and T-shirt or bathing suit for women.

Bring sweats for before and after, keeping in mind that in the summer it is cooler at the beach than inland. A hat or visor and sunglasses are a must, even if you don't wear them when you play. A long-billed hat can halve the eyes' exposure to UV rays and protect the lips, nose, and top of the head.

WHAT ELSE TO BRING

Water

Water is critical. Even if there are drinking fountains at the playing site, they are often far enough away to keep you from drinking as much as you should. If you play several games on a hot day, sweating, breathing, and metabolism will deplete you of fluids. Players out in the sun all day have been known to faint from dehydration.

Sports drinks have gotten a lot of hype for their ability to replace electrolytes—minerals such as potassium, magnesium, and sodium that are lost in sweat. But volleyballers don't sweat as much as, say, marathoners, and if you eat well and drink plenty of water, your electrolytes will be fine.

Food

After a long day of setting and spiking, you'll want food. For athletes, carbohydrates are in, fats are out. Before and after competition, emphasize fruits and vegetables, rice and pasta, bread and cereal.

Go light on the snacks between matches, lest you get sluggish. Try playing on a half-empty tank. In the short run, lack of water will hold you back more than lack of food.

Towel

Some people are driven to dive for balls. Indoor players who do should wear knee and elbow pads for added protection. Sand players who dive often end up coated in a sticky amalgam of sweat and sand. Those in the know call this being "corndogged";

others just call it nasty. Bring a towel or two to wipe off sweat and sand.

Oh yes, and never throw in the towel.

Sunscreen

If you're competing in an outdoor tournament or just having a play date with your friends, forget about working on your tan. A sobering six hundred thousand cases of skin cancer are diagnosed each year in the United States, almost all due to overexposure to the sun's ultraviolet rays. When you play multiple outdoor volleyball games, a relentless sun can be your worst enemy.

Defend yourself with a waterproof, sweatproof, high-SPF (sun-protection factor) sunscreen. Apply it generously and often, beginning at least thirty to forty-five minutes before going out. Studies have shown that people tend to apply only about half the sunscreen the FDA used to determine SPF. Thus SPF 14 effectively becomes SPF 7. It takes at least an ounce to cover the average adult.

Don't forget the lips. They don't tan but they burn. Lip balm with SPF 15 or more is available. Blistex 30 doesn't melt in a hot car or pocket.

Umbrella

As noted above, shade is a valuable commodity at an outdoor tournament. Conserve energy and skin by taking your breaks beneath an umbrella.

Camera

You never know—you may just do something that deserves to be preserved in a photo album. Get a friend to take pictures; you can always destroy them later.

Reading Material

There's plenty of downtime at tournaments. Unless you expect to be riveted by every match, bring books and magazines.

TECHNIQUE

·······································

To excel in volleyball, you need to develop six basic skills: serve, pass, set, block, spike, and tip. Let's look at each in detail.

THE SERVE

Serving a volleyball is much like shooting a basketball free throw in that both offer an opportunity to perform the same physical act the same way every time. The serve is your chance to seize the moment; at no other time in volleyball will you have as much control over what happens—thus the importance of developing proper serving mechanics and holding fast to them. Serving a volleyball is a fairly simple act, and most beginners can develop an accurate, if not powerful, serve by learning the proper way to do it and practicing.

A serve begins every rally of every game. And because a team only scores points when it wins its serve, service skills are critical. If two teams are evenly matched on offense and defense, the one that serves better will usually win.

The serve can set the tone for what follows. Aggressive serving tends to carry over to other phases of the game, and repeated serve-return errors can eradicate the defensive team's momentum and drag them into a grand funk.

The serve can be a great equalizer. You may be less physically imposing than your opponents, but serving from 30 feet behind the net reduces the importance of height and strength. An effective serve can diminish the impact of a potent attacker.

Strive for tactical intelligence and ball control. That is, know where you want to hit the ball, and then hit it there. This puts pressure on the opponents to make a good first pass, an important prerequisite to the set-and-spike.

Your first goal is to learn to serve the ball consistently over the net into the opponents' court. If you hit the ball out-of-bounds or into the net, you lose the serve and your team must then win two rallies in a row to score. But put the ball in play and you give the opponents the first opportunity to misfire. Continue to win your serve and you score points, control play, and share a lot of high-fives.

There are various ways of serving, all of which work sometimes for some players. Although you will no doubt find a favorite style, you would do well to practice all of them, as versatility will make you more effective.

Underhand Serve. The easiest serve to learn and control is the underhand serve. You should be able to put nine out of ten underhand serves in play before attempting other serves.

To start the underhand serve, stand facing the net in the service area. Assume a slight stride position, with the leg opposite your hitting hand slightly forward and your shoulders square to the net. Hold the ball in the nonserving hand, in front of your body about waist high. Your weight should be evenly distributed on both feet.

Your hitting hand will swing back above waist level and then forward to contact the ball. In concert with the arm swing, your weight shifts to the rear foot and then forward to the front foot, lending power to the hit. Just before contact, your holding hand drops away from the ball. Some give the ball a little toss, but in the beginning, this may hurt your accuracy. In any event, by rule you cannot hit the ball while it rests in your hand; it must be released in some fashion.

Hit behind the ball just below its center with the heel of an open hand. See the hand contact the ball, watch the flight of the serve, then move onto the court to field your position.

Underhand Serve Preparation
1. Feet in comfortable, staggered, stride position.
2. Weight evenly distributed.
3. Shoulders square to net.
4. Ball held waist high or lower near center of body.
5. Eyes pick out where you want to hit ball.
6. Firm, open hitting hand.

Figure 2. The underhand serve.

Execution: Server contacts ball with heel of
open hand at waist level as ball-holding hand drops.

Follow-through

Because of its soft trajectory, the underhand delivery is the easiest serve to return. Still, it should remain the choice of beginners until they master one of the advanced serving styles. Even if opponents return your arcing serve, you're in better shape than if you'd hit a powerful serve out-of-bounds. Serving into the net, a sure loser, is the worst of all errors.

Execution
1. Swing hitting arm back and transfer weight to rear foot.
2. Swing hitting arm forward and transfer weight to front foot as ball is contacted.
3. Before and during contact, eyes are on ball.
4. Contact ball with the heel of the hand at about waist level, as hand holding ball drops.
5. Contact ball below center back.
6. Holding hand does not swing forward.
7. Eyes stay on ball through contact.

Aftermath
1. Hitting hand swings forward toward top of net.
2. Weight ends up on front foot.
3. Server moves onto court to defensive position.

Correcting Underhand Serving Errors
- Error: The ball travels up more than forward, failing to reach the net.
  Correction: Hold the ball at waist level or lower; contact the ball just below center back; swing your arm toward the net, not toward the sky; transfer weight from rear to front foot as you contact the ball.
- Error: The ball lacks the power to clear the net.
  Correction: Do not move the holding hand away from your body; contact ball with the heel of your open hand.

Overhand Floater Serve

More powerful, and more difficult to control, are the overhand serves. One, the overhand floater serve, lacks spin and therefore darts through the air like a knuckleball. The floater is especially effective served outdoors into the wind.

The key to proper execution of the overhand floater serve is the toss, which should be in front of your hitting shoulder with sufficient height to allow you to swing your arm and contact the ball at full extension. The toss should impart little or no spin to the ball.

As with the underhand serve, assume a slight stride position, the foot opposite the hitting hand slightly forward, weight evenly distributed, shoulders square to the net. As you toss the ball, draw back the hitting arm so that the elbow is high and the hand is close to the ear.

As your arm swings forward, begin to transfer your weight from the rear foot to the front foot. Keep your eyes on the ball. It's a sharp serve, powered by a quick wrist snap. Contact between the heel of the hand and the ball is brief. To minimize spin, hit just below back center. Change speeds to throw off the opponents' timing.

The erratic movement of the floater—it may rise, drop, break sideways, dart out of bounds suddenly, or drop unexpectedly in-bounds—makes it a difficult serve to control. Practice to find what works best for you, and note the results you get from subtle changes.

Overhand Serve Preparation
1. Comfortable stride position with foot opposite contact hand forward.
2. Weight evenly distributed.
3. Shoulders square to the net.
4. Eyes on ball.
5. Open hitting hand.

Execution
1. With one hand, toss ball close to body ahead of hitting shoulder, imparting little or no spin.

Figure 3. The overhand floater serve.

In order to generate power, the server must rotate his hips and shoulders into the ball.

Execution: Servers should contact the ball with an open hand.

2. Bring arm back with elbow high and hand close to ear.
3. Contact center of ball with heel of open hand.
4. Contact with arm at full extension.
5. Transfer weight onto front foot.
6. Keep eyes on ball through contact.
7. Follow through to target.

Aftermath
1. Weight on front foot.
2. Arm stops after contact with no follow-through after it is in line with target.
3. Move onto court to play defense.

Correcting Overhand Serving Errors
- Error: The serve goes into the net.
  Correction: Make sure the toss is close to the body and not too far out in front.
- Error: The serve goes off to the right.
  Correction: Make sure the toss is in front of the shoulder of your hitting hand and not off to the side of your body.
- Error: The serve lacks power.
  Correction: Use the entire body, shifting your weight from rear to front foot. Increase the speed of the hitting arm. Contact the ball with the heel of the hand, not with the fingers.
- Error: The ball goes too far, beyond the opposite baseline.
  Correction: Toss the ball in front of your body, not directly over your head. Slow down your arm swing slightly. Make contact just below the ball's center back.

Topspin Serve

You execute the topspin serve much like the overhand floater, but with some key differences. Instead of squaring off to the net, turn your shoulders slightly toward the right sideline (right-handers) and point your forward foot toward that net post (fig 4). Toss the ball slightly behind your hitting shoulder. Slightly arch the back and contact the ball with the heel of the hand just above the ball's center back with your arm at full extension, followed immediately

Figure 4. The topspin serve.

Execution: The topspin server must bend his back for power.

Follow-through

by a sharp wrist snap. That causes the fingers to roll over the top of the ball and drives the hitting hand forcibly down to the waist.

By striking this serve hard, you impart forward spin to the ball, causing it to drop, ideally, somewhere in your opponents' court. Because the ball is traveling fast, the receiving team has little time to react. The ball's tendency to drop makes it difficult to judge whether a deep serve will land in or out.

Topspin Serve Preparation
1. Feet in comfortable stride position.
2. Weight evenly distributed.
3. Shoulders and feet angle toward sideline.
4. Eyes on ball toss position.

Execution
1. Toss ball slightly behind hitting shoulder, with little or no spin.
2. Swing hitting arm back, keeping elbow high and hand close to ear.
3. Contact ball with heel of open hand and arm fully extended.
4. Arch back.
5. Snap wrist forcefully, rolling the fingers over top of ball.
6. Keep eyes on ball through contact.

Aftermath
1. Wrist snap forces arm down to waist level.
2. Move onto court to play defense.

Correcting Topspin Serving Errors
- Error: The ball goes into the net.
  Correction: Toss the ball behind the shoulder of your hitting hand.
- Error: The ball goes to the right.
  Correction: Toss the ball in line with your body, not outside your hitting shoulder.
- Error: The ball does not reach the net.
  Correction: Angle body toward sideline to create torque. Swing faster. Contact the ball with the heel of an open hand. Transfer your weight forward at contact.

- Error: The ball flies too deep.
  Correction: Create topspin by contacting the ball near center back and snapping your wrist sharply. Slow down your arm swing.

Jump Serve

This advanced serve is basically a spike from 30 feet away from the net. It demands a high, precise toss to allow the server to contact the ball as high and as far into the court as possible.

A hard jump serve forces your opponents to react quickly, increasing the chances of a passing error. But it also increases the chances of a serving error. Therein lies the classic trade-off. Practice this skill until it feels smooth and natural.

Figure 5. The jump serve.

The jump server jumps well into his own court before contact.

Service Faults

There are three ways to fault during service: (1) serving into the net; (2) serving out-of-bounds; (3) stepping on or over the baseline before contacting the ball.

Serving into the net is perhaps the most frustrating error, because even a slight brush of the net cord shatters any chance of success. But serve a ball that clears the net and is close to a boundary line, and you force the receiving team to make a decision. Good players tend to play the close ball, thereby making it an effective serve.

Strive to hit your serves into the opponents' court. Faulting on a serve is demoralizing becaue it forces your team to win the next rally just to prevent the other team from scoring.

Serving Drills

Ball Toss Placement. The volleyball serve, like the tennis serve, begins with a toss. Although you must toss much higher for an overhand serve than for an underhand one, accuracy is critical in both.

Place a 12-inch-square target—paper or cardboard—on the floor or ground in front of you and between your feet. Stand in an underhand serving position, with the ball at waist level, and let the holding hand drop away. Try to direct the ball so that it hits the target. Practice until you can succeed nine times out of ten.

For the overhand drill, lift the ball with a smooth, vertical motion, keeping the hand in contact with the ball as long as possible. At release, your arm should be almost straight. The ball should not rise from the hand too far (some coaches suggest 6 to 8 inches), because a high throw will turn small tossing mistakes into big ones. Again, practice until you are successful hitting the target nine tries out of ten.

Wall Serve. Stand in a serving position about 30 feet from a wall upon which is painted or taped a horizontal line at proper net height. Toss and serve the ball above the line on the wall. Try for nine good underhand serves out of ten attempts, then nine good overhand serves out of ten attempts.

Partner to Partner. You and a partner stand on opposite sides of the court, each about 20 feet from the net. Serve the ball cleanly over the net so that your partner can catch the ball without moving more than a step in any direction. Move around the court and practice until you are successful at least seven tries out of ten.

End-Line Serve. Hit repeated serves from the service area toward the opposite baseline, trying to come as close as possible and still keep the ball in. See how many times in a row you can succeed.

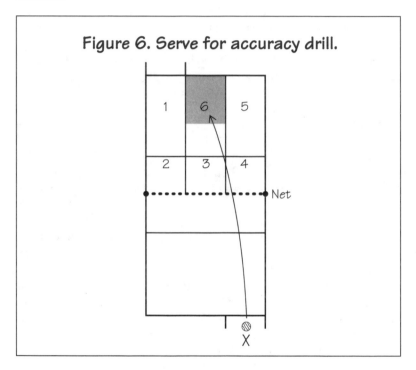

Figure 6. Serve for accuracy drill.

Serve for Accuracy

a) Place a flat marker approximately 10 feet square on one of the six rotational positions on the opposite side of the court. From the proper service area, try to hit clean serves onto the marker. Move the marker and practice hitting the other five target areas. Serve ten to each position, trying to hit the target five or more times.

b) Mark off the six positions, as shown in fig 6. Hit ten serves to each position and score as follows: Award three points for hitting the primary target; two points for hitting the spot next to and just as long as the primary target; one point for hitting one of the other positions; no points for a fault. Try for twenty points on ten serves.

THE PASS

The receive-set-spike style of offense that is practiced by quality volleyball teams depends on a high, accurate pass to a setter. A bad pass, like a bad foundation, causes the whole edifice to crumble. Even accomplished spikers need a good set, and setters need a good pass—thus the importance of developing good passing skills. Passes can be made from below the waist, the *bump* or *forearm pass,* or from above the waist, the *overhead pass* or *volley.*

The Bump, or Forearm Pass

The bump is used to receive serves, to play balls at waist level and below, and to play balls off the net. If you are scrambling or diving to reach an errant ball, the bump is usually the shot of choice. It can be made from almost any angle, and may even be hit back over your head.

> "**The most important play in volleyball? It's got to be the pass. Some teams that are strong at the net—spiking and blocking—can overcome weaker passing. But it's rare."**
> —**Rudy Suwara, assistant coach of the 1996 U.S. Olympic team**

If your team receives serve, the first skill it must execute is the *forearm pass.* Although you often have more control with the fingertip overhead pass, referees will call a fault if you don't bump the serve. Open hands are simply not strong enough to handle a ball hit with great force, and unless you have perfect timing you will be guilty of a hold. The biggest difference between "jungle ball" and disciplined volleyball is that good players bump serves and spikes, whereas the untutored usually hit with upturned, open hands.

Another difference is that beginners typically direct the ball over the net on the first or second hit. Ideally, the first hit should absorb much of the force of the ball, resulting in a soft, easy-to-handle pass to a setting teammate.

Bump Ready Position. A good starting position will help you get a good jump (fig 7). Stay high and relaxed, with the hands on or near the body. Bend at the waist, but only slightly. To maintain good balance, keep the feet side-by-side and spread somewhat wider than the shoulders. The knees should be slightly bent, with the weight on the front part of the feet, allowing you to push off with your toes. A slight shift in weight from side to side or up and down can improve balance.

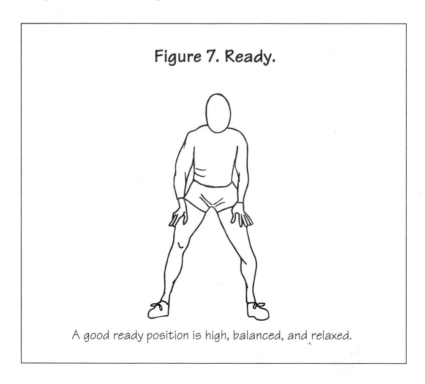

Figure 7. Ready.

A good ready position is high, balanced, and relaxed.

From this position, scrutinize the server to see where she's facing and where she tosses. Many right-handed servers toss to the left because they're releasing the ball with their left hand; that usually means they will serve crosscourt. Floaters are tossed lower and out front, and hit flat with no wrist snap; topspin and jump serves are tossed higher and are contacted above the head.

Technique. Once you see the ball coming toward you, move the lower body in advance of the upper body. Resist the temptation to reach out early with the arms—running like that is awkward and slow. As you slide to the anticipated passing spot, carry most of your weight on the front part of the feet and keep your eyes unwaveringly on the ball.

When it's all you can do to reach the ball, you have to dig—that is, hit the ball below the waist. Pursue the ball in your area relentlessly, beat it to its spot, and be prepared to dive.

> **When adjusting to the ball, the forearm passer:**
>
> - **Moves the feet first.**
> - **Hops into passing position**
> - **Places the feet:**
>   - **side-by-side**
>   - **wider than the shoulders**
>   - **flat on the floor**

When you see that the ball is going to arrive nearby, execute a series of quick bounces to adjust your position. For balance, keep your feet side-by-side and spread, arms comfortably away from your body. If the ball takes you a step or two to the side, the bounce becomes a side step. Lead with the foot nearer the passing site and follow with a skip-step. Finish the sequence with the feet side-by-side, ready to pass or make another side step. Both the bounce and the side step allow you to face the ball while moving and to stop easily.

To reach a ball that is more than two or three steps away, you should cross and run. As with the side step, lead with the foot nearer the passing site, but then turn both body and feet toward the ball, rotating the hips 90 degrees. Your second step makes the crossover, and now you are running. Running is obviously faster than side-stepping, but stopping is more difficult.

Once you reach the ball, your best chance to stop is with a little hop. The hop turns your body back toward the hitter and places your feet in a side-by-side position. Hold your arms in front of your body, knees bent, and absorb the force of the ball. Your outstretched arms are now parallel to your thighs. Use a poking action, rather than a big arm swing.

Figure 8. The forearm pass, or bump.

The passer uses a short arm swing.

When executing the bump, your hands should be linked, with the length of your thumbs touching and parallel. Rotate your elbows toward one another, so that the soft, flat insides of your forearms face the ceiling. The platform formed by your hands and arms should be as seamless as possible.

To assure accurate forearm passes, follow these suggestions:

- Join your hands. Many coaches believe that interlocking the fingers at the first knuckle leaves the forearm muscles relaxed, allowing a quicker response.
- Lock your elbows so that your arms do not bend. This allows them to work as one.
- Roll your forearms outward, turning the flat part toward the ball.
- Hold your forearms as close together as possible to eliminate double-hits.

If you move to the ball well and get in proper position, the bump is a relatively easy skill to learn. The difficulty is that, unless you're a linebacker, you probably haven't used your forearms in any other sport. The tendency you must fight, then, is to bump with your hands.

Bump Over. The *bump over* is a forearm pass that plays the ball over the net. It is usually a mistake or at best a last resort, used when the offensive team has no other way to keep the ball in play. It is often dictated by a bad pass or a defensive dig on the second shot, which forces a desperation bump over on a team's third and final touch.

> **Try to serve to the opponents' weakest passer, even if that person is a good setter or spiker. A bad opening pass will increase the chances of a weak set and hit.**

When you are hustling to make a saving play, the bump over can be a good shot, as it seldom results in a foul (unlike the alternative—an underhand, open-hand lift) and allows enough control to keep the ball in play. It may be the only shot available when the third and final shot must be made from deep in your own court. The bump over can be made from almost any angle, including over your head with your back to the net. Although it is not much of an offensive threat, it can prolong the rally, giving the opponents the next chance to make a mistake.

Bump Preparation
1. Interlock fingers at first knuckle, or cradle fingers of one hand in fingers of the other.
2. Press heels of hands together, thumbs parallel and touching.
3. Roll the forearms out and lock the elbows.
4. Assume a balanced stance, feet shoulder-width apart.
5. Bend at knees and waist, and push hips to the rear.
6. Forearms are parallel to thighs.
7. Back is straight.
8. Head is steady, and eyes are on ball.

Execution
1. Last-moment adjustments enable you to receive ball one-third to one-half of the way between wrists and elbows.

2. Strike ball with short arm swing, a poking motion.
3. Arms stop at around 45-degree angle to the floor.
4. Angle arm platform toward your target.
5. Hold body and head still.

Aftermath
1. Hands remain linked.
2. Soften the hit by pulling arms back slightly after contact.
3. Arms stay below shoulders.
4. Eyes follow ball to target.

Correcting Bump Errors
- Error: Your arms are too high when you contact the ball or complete the follow-through.
  Correction: Let the ball drop to waist level or below before contact. Poke at the ball to avoid following through.
- Error: You reach low balls by bending at the waist instead of at the knees, causing low, hard passes.
  Correction: Bend your knees and keep your back straight, more vertical than horizontal. Also, be prepared to bend at the elbows—known as the "J" stroke—if that is necessary to hit the ball up.
- Error: The ball does not go where you intend it to go.
  Correction: Check that your weight shifts toward the intended target and ends up on your forward foot. Your body should be inclined forward. Keep the arms, hands, and thumbs parallel.
- Error: The ball contacts your upper arms or torso, resulting in double-hits and little or no control.
  Correction: Keep the arms parallel to the thighs and adjust your position so that you contact the ball away from your body.

Bump Passing Drills

Passing a Held Ball. Have a partner loosely hold a ball out toward you about waist height. Using the bump technique, hit

One way to check if the bump is being executed properly is to watch the spin on the ball as it comes off your arms. Bumped correctly, the ball should have little or no spin. Spin suggests that you are swinging your arms too much, rather than lifting them with the elbows locked.

the ball out of your partner's hands so that it travels over her head.

Partner Pass. Have a partner pass you a ball. Using the bump technique, pass it back to him so that he can catch it by taking no more than one step in any direction. When you can consistently succeed nine times out of ten, increase the distance between you by 5 feet. And so on.

Continuous Bumping. Gently toss a ball to yourself and use your forearms to keep it in the air. Try to bump it ten, twenty, twenty-five times in a row while staying in a 10-foot square. Increase the height until you can comfortably bump the ball 8 to 10 feet in the air.

Passing to Target. An "opponent" tosses a ball over the net, and you bump it to a teammate near the center of the net (position 3), the ideal spot for a setter. When you can succeed eight times out of ten, have the opponent toss the ball so that you have to move for it.

Bump for Accuracy. Stand in one of the back-row positions, while a partner stands on the attack line of the same side. As the partner tosses the ball to either your left or right, move to receive and bump toward one of the front-row squares. Your passes should reach a height about 2 feet above the net. Hit ten to court position 3 and note your results.

Overhead Pass

The overhead pass is the most efficient way to handle a high, easy ball. Players use the overhead pass to move the ball to a teammate, usually a setter, and rarely to return the ball to the opponents. You should be able to execute this pass either forward or backward with approximately the same style of delivery. Move your body to avoid steering the ball sideways, which is usually a fault.

The overhead pass can be used by a player receiving any ball that arrives above shoulder level and with little speed. Don't let those balls drop to forearm-pass level, because a well-executed overhead pass offers greater control.

Adopt the ready position: square to the target in a slight stride, feet shoulder-width apart, knees bent, and your hands about 6 to 8 inches in front of your forehead with your thumbs pointing toward your eyes. In this way, your thumbs form a window, through which you see the ball.

As you contact the ball, extend your arms and legs, transferring your weight in the intended direction of the pass. In this way, the entire body imparts force to the ball, allowing you greater height and distance. Only the upper two joints of the fingers and thumbs actually touch the ball.

Overhead Pass Preparation
1. Feet are in a comfortable stride position.
2. Body moves to ball and squares to target.
3. Arms and legs are slightly bent.
4. Hands are positioned 6–8 inches above the forehead.
5. Eyes follow the ball through the window formed by the hands.

Execution
1. Hands mold to ball.
2. Upper two joints of fingers and thumbs contact ball's lower back.
3. Arms and legs extend toward target.
4. Transfer weight toward target.

Aftermath
1. Arms are fully extended, with hands pointing toward the target.
2. Weight is shifted toward target.
3. Move in direction of ball.

Correcting Overhead Passing Errors
- Error: The ball contacts your palms, and you are called for a held ball.

Correction: Separate your hands, and spread your fingers. Contact the ball with only the upper two joints of your fingers and thumbs.
- Error: Your passes spin too much.
Correction: Give the ball immediate impetus, rather than letting it roll off your hands.
- Error: You have trouble directing the ball toward the target.
Correction: Position your shoulders square to the target. Let both hands do an equal amount of work, rather than favoring one over the other.
- Error: The ball travels up rather than out toward the target.
Correction: Contact the ball at its lower back, not its bottom. Extend your limbs and transfer body weight toward the target.
- Error: Your overhead passes lack height or power.
Correction: Get lower by bending at the knees. Move your arms faster. Prior to and during contact, extend your arms and legs and shift your weight forward. Use the whole body, especially when the ball has to travel a long ways.

Overhead Passing Drills

Pass-Bounce-Pass. Overhead pass a well-inflated ball high into the air, let it hit the floor and bounce, then pass it again after it reaches its apex. Try to keep the ball in a controlled area the size of half of one side of the court. See how many in a row you can pass without missing. Break your own record.

Partner Toss and Pass. Have a partner toss a ball high and easy toward you. Overhead pass the ball back so the partner can catch it without moving more than one step. As you improve, incrementally increase the height of the toss and the distance between you and your partner. Keep track of your results.

Free Ball Passing. You need four players for this drill. A tosser stands on one side of the net, near the attack line; a blocker, setter, and passer stand on the other side of the net. The passer sets up near the net, hands in front of his shoulders, fingers spread. The setter stands near the attack line.

The tosser yells "free" and tosses the ball over the net near the attack line. Upon hearing "free," which tells the receiving team that no block is needed, the setter moves to center net, and the passer slides back to the attack line. The passer receives the ball and overhead passes it to a teammate. Passes should be 2–3 feet higher than the top of the net and within one step of the setter. Work on it until you can nail eight out of ten.

THE SET

The set is an overhead pass, usually on the second touch, that positions the ball for the final attack. The height of the set, which can be hit either in front of or behind the setter, can vary depending upon the type of set desired. The ideal set should be at least 2 feet off the net, allowing the attacker to hit the ball without contacting the net. The best spikers in the world will be rendered ineffective by a poor set.

The setter normally takes a position on the right side of the court, near the net and facing the left sideline. From there, the setter can execute three basic types of sets: high outside set, quick set, and back-set. All three require the same preparation so as not to telegraph what is coming.

The ideal high, outside set, at least 6 feet higher than the top of the net, is hit so that it would land on the left sideline if it went untouched. The attacker, of course, must adjust to the precise position of this set.

In the quick set, the setter sets directly in front of herself and 1 to 2 feet higher than the top of the net. The attacker approaches the net in front of the setter and jumps as, or before, the setter contacts the ball; thus it is critical that the setter set the ball accurately for the attacker.

The back-set demands the same basic technique as the front-set. You contact the ball in the same place—in front of your forehead—but the back-setter arches his back and directs the ball over his head. His shoulders and arms move backward while his hips move forward. The back-set doesn't travel quite as high as the high outside set, peaking about 5 feet above the top of the net.

To review the preparation, execution, and aftermath of the set, consult the section on the overhead pass.

Figure 9. The front set.

Preparation: The setter's
elbows are held very wide.

Execution

Follow-through

Figure 10. The back-set (side view).

The back-setter's shoulders and arms move
backward while her hips move forward.

Setting Drills

Short Pass, Back Pass, Long Pass. Three players stand in
a line about 10 feet apart. Two face one direction, with the third
player facing the other two. The third player initiates the action
with an overhead pass to the middle player, who back-sets the
ball to the last player, who long passes the ball back to the
starter. See how many three-pass sequences you can complete.

Pass, Move, Back-Set. Face a partner, overhead pass the
ball to her, then run to a spot behind her. Your partner receives
your pass, passes once or twice to herself, back-sets it to you, then
turns and faces you. After receiving her pass, you overhead pass

it back to her, completing the sequence. Try for 10 consecutive pass and back-set combinations.

Pass and Circle. As in the last drill, face a partner and overhead pass the ball to her. Then run all the way around her and back to your starting point. As you circumnavigate your partner, she keeps the ball in play with overhead passes to herself. When you finally reach your starting point, your partner overhead passes back to you, completing the sequence. Keep the ball going and try for 10 consecutive pass-and-go sequences.

THE BLOCK

Once you progress to the intermediate level of play, spiking and blocking become integral parts of the game. The block at the net, then, is the first line of defense against your opponents' attack. If the other side has an effective setter and spiker, and you lack blockers, the game will be a mismatch. The alternative to blocking—backing off the net, reading the attacker, and then digging with four or five players—has scant chance of success against a good attacker.

Your ultimate goal as a blocker is to prevent the ball from entering your side of the court. Even if your block returns the ball to the attackers' side in a nice, easy arc, you still force your opponents to reset their attack. The longer they play the ball, the greater the chance they will err. And even if your block gets only a piece of the ball, you may deflect it high onto your own side of the court, allowing your teammates more time to play a less forceful ball.

In a *single block,* only one player blocks at a time. Good teams will often join two or three players in what is called a *multiple block.* The wider the block, the less court the remaining players must cover.

Block Ready Position

Blockers should set up close to the net, feet side-by-side and about shoulder-width apart, weight forward. Hold your hands comfortably above your shoulders, palms forward, back straight. Spread your fingers, and bend your knees slightly.

Watch as your opponents' attack develops. Every movement on the other side of the net offers clues about what will happen next. A setter whose hands are way out in front of her body is going to front-set fast and low; if she arches her back before contacting the ball, she is going to back-set. If she sets inside, the hitter will usually go crosscourt.

Technique

When you decide a block is imminent, bend at the waist and sag into a crouch, keeping the back straight and the face forward. When the knees near a right angle, pause, ready to jump. Practice to see what depth of knee bend pushes you the highest.

When it's time to block, come out of the crouch, push off and leap vertically, arms straight up and firm from shoulders to fingertips. Fingers are spread and thumbs angle upward less than a ball-width apart, preventing the ball from passing between your hands (fig 11). Keep your hands and arms less than a ball's diameter from the net to assure that the ball does not fall between yourself and the net. To maximize the area you protect, reach across the net into the opponents' court. Penetrating the plane of the net is both legal and effective. (You're not allowed to hit the ball, as opposed to blocking it, before it breaks the plane of the net.)

The timing of the jump should be based on the depth of the set; that is, the farther the set is from the net, the later the blocker jumps. To defend a set made near the plane of the net, the blocker might jump a nanosecond later than the spiker; if the set falls 2 feet from the net, the blocker might jump as the spiker's hitting arm starts back; to block a set 3 feet from the net, the blocker might jump as the spiker's hitting arm moves forward into the ball; if it's a deep set, the blocker might jump after the spiker contacts the ball.

> **The most common blocking error is focusing on the ball to the exclusion of the opposing attacker. After the set reaches its apex, your eyes should pick up the hitter and read his body language.**

The blocker who is too short or who cannot jump high enough to reach across the net without contacting it should resort to soft blocks. The soft blocker angles his hands backward, toward his own court, with the heels of his hands pointed toward the spiker's contact point with the ball. He tries to slow the ball, angling it upward so that one of his own backcourt players can handle it.

Even if you have poor position, you may be able to soft block. Your mere presence may distract the hitter, or your hands may be in the right place at the right time. Sometimes good things happen by accident.

Figure 11. The single block.

When the blocker's knees are near a right angle, he pauses, ready to jump.

The blocker jumps vertically, his arms straight and firm from shoulder to fingertip.

The blocker lands with knees bent and hands near his face to avoid touching the net.

Outside Blocker

The outside blocker—the one closest to the sideline—should angle the palms of his hands slightly toward the center of the court. Called blocking *outside-in,* it reduces the area protected by the block but lowers the chances of deflecting the ball out of bounds.

Figure 12. The multiple block.

Note the formidable wall formed by two blockers.

The team's defensive strategy dictates whether the outside blocker sets up near the sideline, close to the center, or somewhere in between. Strategy also determines whether the blocker protects the sideline or the center. To protect the line, the blocker places her inside hand in front of the ball; to protect the angle, she positions her outside hand in front of the ball. If the opponent's set is high and near the center net, both outside blockers can join the middle blocker, forming a triple block.

Middle Blocker

The middle blocker must be alert for the quick attack, which usually comes in the middle. Read the setter and try to anticipate where the ball will be set. If you see the quick attack coming, jump with the quick hitter and try to stuff the smash (block it to the floor). You want to stop the middle attack without sacrificing the opportunity to help out near the sidelines. When the set goes to a sideline, sidestep to join an outside blocker.

As the middle blocker, you should plant your foot 4–6 inches (10–15 centimeters) from your teammate's inside foot. Like the outside blocker, shift your gaze to the spiker as the set peaks. Jump vertically to avoid drifting into your teammate, and adjust the position of your hands as you read the direction of the attack. Keep in mind that experienced spikers often avoid hitting straight ahead. As the middle blocker, if you see the opposing outside hitter intends to angle the ball inside the block, reach to the inside with either the inside hand or both hands.

In an effective double-block, both blockers are close enough so that the attacker must hit over or around four outstretched arms. If the middle blocker arrives late, she can soft block; later still, she can extend one hand; too late, she can cover, or back up, a possible deflection.

Block Preparation
1. Wait close to net.
2. Watch opposing setter.
3. Keep hands at shoulder level, palms out, fingers spread.
4. After set, focus on opposing attacker.
5. Adjust position one-half body width to attacker's hitting side.

Execution
1. Time jump by set's distance from net.
2. Extend arms above top of the net.
3. Reach across net into opponents' court.
4. After block, withdraw hands so they don't touch the net.
5. Land on both feet.

Aftermath
1. Bend the knees to cushion landing.
2. Turn and find ball.

Correcting Blocking Errors
- Error: You jump to block too early.
  Correction: Watch the opposing setter to intuit where the ball will be set; then watch the attacker to gain proper timing; wait to jump until after the attacker jumps.
- Error: Your fingers are closed.
  Correction: Spread your fingers wide and point your thumbs toward the ceiling.
- Error: You miss blocks because you're lined up face-to-face with the attacker.
  Correction: Shift your position one-half body width to the attacker's hitting side.
- Error: As the joining blocker, you bang into a teammate setting the block.
  Correction: Use peripheral vision to determine your teammate's position; jump vertically.
- Error: The ball contacts your hands and drops to your side of the court.
  Correction: Square your shoulders to the net; jump close to the net without contacting it.
- Error: You land hard with straight legs.
  Correction: Bend your knees and sag into the landing, softening the blow.

Blocking Drills

Toss and Block. Two players are needed: a tosser on one side of the court, a blocker on the other side. The tosser, using a two-handed overhead motion, jumps and attempts to throw the ball over the net in a downward motion. The blocker jumps and attempts to block the ball before it passes the plane of the net. The goal is for the blocked ball to land in the opposite court. Strive for success six times out of ten.

Blind Blocking. Three players participate: tosser and blocker on one side, spiker on the other. The tosser, who is behind the blocker, throws the ball over the net, high and relatively close to it. The spiker jumps and spikes the ball, aiming for the blocker, who leaps and tries to stuff it back into the opponents' court. A blocker who is successful four times out of ten is doing well.

Double-Block. Four players participate: tosser and attacker on one side, two blockers on the other side. One blocker stands near the center of the net, the other near a sideline.

The tosser tosses the ball high and outside to the attacker. The attacker, starting where the attack line intersects a sideline, approaches and spikes the ball over the net. The middle blocker joins the outside blocker to form a double-block. Blockers should concentrate on jumping vertically and simultaneously.

THE ATTACK

In the absence of unforced errors by your opponents, you will score points by attacking. There are three main prongs of attack in volleyball: spike, half-spike, and tip. Watch your setter for clues on what to do. If your team gives your setter a bad pass, don't expect a great set. If the setter is on the other side of the court, look for an inside set. As you approach, read the blockers and the defenders.

The Spike

Like batting in baseball, spiking is volleyball's glamour skill. It is the favorite activity of many beginners, often to the exclusion of other facets of the game. There's a reason for this: Spiking a volleyball is one of the most dynamic acts in all of sports. A spiked volleyball, when struck with proper technique and timing, can rocket across the net at seventy miles per hour. What other sport allows you to jump as high as you can and hit a ball as hard as you can—with your hand?

When executing the hard-driven spike, contact the ball with the heel of an open, cupped hand. The wrist snaps forward forcibly, imparting topspin, which causes the ball to drop.

Your success at spiking will depend in large part on your ability to disguise your intentions. For a high set, start at the attack line, about 10 feet from the net. Start balanced, with your knees bent, facing the spot where you expect the set to go, eyes riveted

Figure 13. The spike.

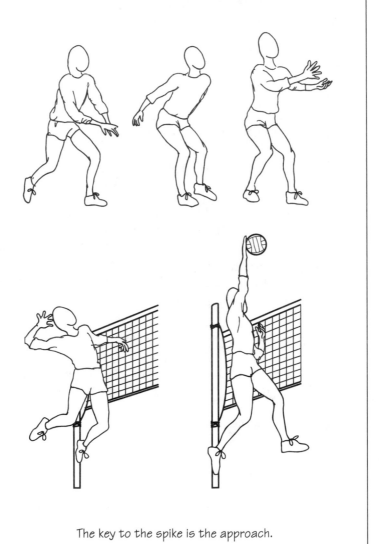

The key to the spike is the approach.

on the ball. As the ball reaches its apex, move toward it. Approach the net with as few steps as possible, using the arms to increase speed.

Step aggressively with the left leg as the right arm swings up (right-handers), a powerful lead to the plant and leap. Sometimes called the adjusting step, it is essentially a one-legged broad jump into a squat position, a buildup for the vertical leap to follow.

Finish with a hop onto both feet, or plant the right foot and close with the left. Plant the heels first and roll onto the front of the foot, transforming forward momentum into upward momentum. Swing the arms back and away from your body, like a bird spreading its wings. As you leave the ground, your arms sweep forward.

> To visualize a successful spike, break it down into three parts: (1) the timing of the approach; (2) the contact in front of the hitting shoulder; (3) the quick, powerful wrist snap. Two common spiking errors are beginning the approach too soon, thus losing momentum, and contacting the ball behind the hitting shoulder.

The nonhitting arm reaches high, framing the ball for the other hand. The hitting arm stops its forward sweep at the shoulder and draws back, much like an archer pulling back his bow. Just before contact, the elbow is high, the hand close to the ear, the forearm parallel to the ground. The drawing back of the hitting hand rotates the shoulders about 45 degrees. You are cocked and ready to explode through the ball.

Spike Preparation
1. Wait on attack line.
2. Watch setter.
3. Weight forward.
4. Anticipate approach to net.

Execution
1. Eyes shift from setter to ball.
2. Begin approach to net when ball reaches its peak, about halfway between setter and spiker.
3. Reach takeoff point in as few steps as possible.
4. Finish approach with either a hop or a heel plant with one foot and a close with the other.
5. Swing arms back to waist height.
6. Swing arms forward and high.
7. Contact ball above and in front of hitting shoulder.
8. Contact with heel of open hand.
9. Contact center back of ball.
10. Contact with full arm extension.
11. Snap wrist forward with force.

Aftermath
1. Keep eyes on ball through contact.
2. Hand follows ball toward target.
3. Land on both feet.
4. Sag into landing.

Correcting Spike Errors
- Error. The ball goes into the net.
  Correction: Contact the ball only slightly in front of your hitting shoulder. The greater the horizontal distance between shoulder and ball, the farther the hand travels before contact and the more likely the ball will be driven into the net.
- Error: You have to stop your approach and wait for the ball, losing momentum and occasionally even overrunning the set.
  Correction: Delay your approach until the ball reaches its apex.
- Error: You contact the net.
  Correction: Plant your heels to shift horizontal momentum to vertical momentum. (Of course, the fault also may be caused by a set that is too close to the net.)
- Error: Your spike tends to fly deep out-of-bounds.
  Correction: Jump a bit farther back. Contact the ball in

front of your hitting shoulder. Snap your wrist sharply, rolling your hand over the top of the ball and imparting topspin that causes the ball to drop.

- Error: Your jump lacks Michael Jordan height.
  Correction: Everyone's jump lacks Michael Jordan's height. To get higher, though, plant your heels to convert horizontal movement to vertical movement; swing both arms forcibly forward and upward; push off with the front part of the feet.

The Tip

The tip is a soft, arcing hit that drops close to the net. It is the blooper ball of volleyball, a change of pace designed to evade a leaping blocker who, intent on repelling a hard-driven spike, watches helplessly as the ball falls softly nearby. Even teams with dominant spikers should mix in tips to throw the opponents off balance.

> **Most tip errors are caused by poor timing or improper hand position.**

The approach for spike and tip should be indistinguishable. At contact, gently tap the ball with the last two finger joints, arm fully extended and slightly ahead of the hitting shoulder. Contact the ball slightly below center back. Direct the ball upward just enough so that it clears the blocker and then drops quickly to the floor. Return to the floor with a two-footed landing.

Tip Preparation
1. Wait on attack line.
2. Watch the setter.
3. Weight forward.
4. Anticipate approach to net.

Execution
1. Eyes shift from setter to ball.
2. Begin approach to net when ball reaches its peak.
3. Reach takeoff point in as few steps as possible.

Figure 14. The tip.

The tip is a soft fingertip push of the ball from a spike approach.

4. Finish approach with either a hop or a heel plant with one foot and a close with the other.
5. Swing arms back to waist height.
6. Swing arms forward and high.
7. Contact ball above and in front of hitting shoulder.
8. Contact with last two finger joints of all five fingers.
9. Contact lower back half of ball.
10. Contact with full arm extension.

Aftermath
1. Keep eyes on ball through contact.

2. Hand follows through in direction of tip, then drops to the waist.
3. Land on both feet.
4. Bend knees and sag into the landing.

Correcting Tipping Errors

- Error: You have to stop your approach and wait for the ball, losing momentum and occasionally even overrunning the set.
  Correction: Delay your approach until the ball reaches its apex.
- Error: The ball goes into the net.
  Correction: Contact the ball only slightly in front of your hitting shoulder. The greater the horizontal distance between shoulder and ball, the farther the hand travels before contact and the more likely the ball will be driven into the net.
- Error: The ball does not clear the block.
  Correction: Contact the back lower half of the ball with your arm fully extended.
- Error: You contact the net.
  Correction: Plant your heels to change horizontal momentum to vertical momentum. (Of course, the fault may be caused by a set that is too close to the net.)
- Error: You tip the ball too high, giving opponents a chance to reach it.
  Correction: Contact the ball earlier, before it reaches your hitting shoulder.
- Error: You have trouble putting the ball where you want it to go.
  Correction: Position your body behind the ball, not off to the side.
- Error: You get called for too many held-ball faults.
  Correction: Avoid trying to steer the ball by changing the angle of your hitting hand after contact. That causes your hand to be in contact with the ball too long. It also looks amateurish, making it a favorite call of referees.

Off-Speed Spike

In between the spike and the tip is the off-speed spike, which is executed the same way as a tip—until contact. Hit the off-speed with the heel of an open hand cutting into the center back of the ball. At contact, the wrist snaps and the fingers roll over the top of the ball, imparting topspin that causes the ball to drop. The arm swing is slower than for the spike.

The Dump

The dump is a surprise tip by the setter, usually on the second team touch. It can catch the opponents off guard, especially if the dumper camouflages her intentions, making the dump look like a routine set.

To execute a dump, hold the hands in a setting position and let the ball fall toward your forehead. As the ball nears the hands, quickly raise the left hand, turning the palm toward the net. With the pads of the fingers, contact the side—not the bottom—of the ball. Add a smooth wrist snap to drive the ball over the net. The right hand does not change position during the dump.

Attack Drills

Spike against Wall. Stand 10 feet from a wall. Spike the ball into the floor, so that it bounces sharply off the floor, rebounds off the wall, and returns to you on the fly. Spike it over and over, working on wrist snap and timing to increase power.

Approach and Throw. Holding the ball, start at the attack line and approach the net, as you would for a spike. Jump and throw the ball forcefully over the net, using a two-hand overhead motion with a wrist snap. Attempt to hit the front two-thirds of the court. Have a partner retrieve the ball for you. Try for seven good tosses out of ten without hitting the net.

Bounce to Target. As in the last drill, hold the ball at the attack line, with a retrieving partner on the other side of the net. Bounce the ball hard to the floor, jump, and spike the rebound over the net. Try to hit half or more within the boundaries of the opponents' court.

International player Bryan Ivie's five common hitting errors:

1. Ineffective approach. Watch the set carefully, and use proper footwork to get to the ball. Get your feet to the ball first with a three-step approach, using your arms to explode upward.
2. Attacking the wrong blocker. When facing a double-block, attack the weaker blocker, usually but not always the shorter of the two.
3. Dropping your elbow. Try to hit as high as possible, with your arm extended. Look up through the ball and swing when it's at its highest point.
4. Approaching too early. Approaching the net before you see where the set is going can leave you under the ball instead of behind it. Start your approach with a small, slow step and continue to go slow until you know your destination, then speed up. If you start too fast and then have to slow down, it's hard to regain momentum.
5. Trying to be too perfect. Cut down on hitting errors by aiming your hits 1 or 2 feet in-bounds instead of trying to hit a boundary line.

Tip to Target. Three players participate: a setter and attacker on one side, a blocker on the other side. The attacker starts at the attack line, the setter is near the net, and the blocker stands on a chair on the other side of the net. Place three or four numbered targets on the blocker's side, between net and attack line.

The setter tosses or sets the ball high to the outside of the court. The attacker approaches and tips around or over the blocker, aiming for the target that corresponds to the number called out by the setter at the last moment. Learn to handle a wide variety of sets with the same arm swing.

Off-Speed Spike to Center Target. Place a 10-foot-square target at center court so that the attack line bisects it. Attackers should hit spikes and off-speed spikes aimed at that target from both the left and right sides of the court. Keep track of your results.

Spike to Deep Target. This drill calls for two players, a setter and a spiker. The setter stands near center net, and the spiker is on the attack line near either sideline. Place two 10-foot-square targets in the deep corners of the opponents' court.

The spiker passes the ball to the setter, who sets back to the spiker. Without jumping, the spiker spike-hits the ball over the net to either of the two large target areas. Try to improve to the point where you can succeed five times out of ten with each target.

STRATEGY

....

Volleyball strategy begins with the three-touch sequence: receive, set, hit. Its purpose is to convert your opponents' serve or attack into your own attack. Too many beginning teams neglect one or two of those touches, but hitting the ball back and forth across the net with only one contact per side is boring and nonproductive.

Once you are committed to the three-touch sequence, introduce strategic thinking into the following areas of your game.

THE LINEUP

Strategic thinking should begin before the ball is even put in play. An effective *lineup*, the order in which the players serve, can maximize a team's strengths and minimize its weaknesses. Conversely, putting together a bad lineup gives the edge to your opponents.

If your team serves to begin the game, right-back serves first, right-front second. If you receive serve to start the game, right-front serves first, after side-out and rotation. After the coin flip, position your best server to give her first crack. Arrange the two best setters three stations apart, so that one of them is always in the front row; likewise the two best attackers. The best attacker should start left-front so that her first three stations are in the front row. If the attacker is right-handed, the best setter starts middle-front so that she can set the attacker *on-hand* (closer to her dominant hand). The best passers should start in the back-court.

Devising the perfect lineup may be complicated by the fact that your best server is also your best attacker; or perhaps your best passer is the best—or only—setter. The lineup becomes a

Figure 15. Position of players on the court.

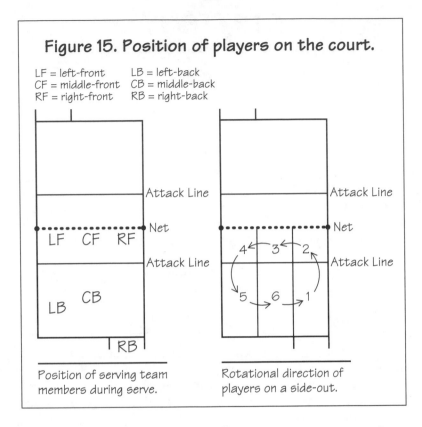

LF = left-front   LB = left-back
CF = middle-front CB = middle-back
RF = right-front   RB = right-back

Position of serving team members during serve.

Rotational direction of players on a side-out.

balancing act, a trade-off, and the coach or captain may have some tough decisions to make. Writing the players' names on scraps of paper and moving them about a paper court divided into six sections can help you visualize the possibilities.

SERVING

If you know your opponents, the obvious strategy may be to serve to the weakest player or the one against whom you've had the most success. But somehow it never seems to be that simple. Maybe that weak player is a poor spiker but a strong digger; or maybe he just had a bad day when you faced him. If you have a complete dossier on your opponents, serve away from the best passer.

If you don't know your opponents, study them as the match goes on. Who is the best passer, setter, spiker? Who looks tired? Whom are you having success against?

One way to develop a serving strategy is to consider what your opponents do that causes *you* problems. What serves put you at the greatest disadvantage? Your list might include the following:

- floater serves that change direction in midflight
- serves that make you move to pass
- serves that bring sun, wind, or lighting into play
- serves that cause indecision between partners as to whose play it is
- serves that have a lot of top- or sidespin
- serves that look like a blur

RECEIVING SERVE

The most common receiving formation has five players bunched rather tightly in a W, with the sixth player, the setter, at center net (fig 16). When players are not accustomed to switching during play, middle-front should always try to set. Note that in proper serve-receive, middle-back moves forward to take a position in line with left- and right-forward.

Beginners are not comfortable being bunched like this. Middle-back wants to play too deep, and left-front and right-front creep forward and wide, taking them out of position to receive most serves. Bunching the players in the backcourt provides the optimum positioning for receiving serve, allowing them to pass without moving far.

Of course, the W formation is not static; it moves as the situation dictates. From the point of view of the receiving team, if the serve takes flight from the left side of the opposite baseline, it will, more often than not, pass over the left side of the net; so knowledgeable teams will shift their W slightly to the left. The left-front is now less than 3 feet from the left sideline, the right-front more than 3 feet from the right sideline. The back-row players are in the seams—between the players immediately in front and about 5 feet from the baseline. A serve reaching them above the waist should be out-of-bounds.

Figure 16. Receiving serve.

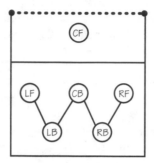

The beginning serve-receive formation arranges its passers in a "W." The setter stays at the net.

The receivers stand, ready to move quickly.

With the leftward shift of the W, the receiving team's right sideline becomes a tempting target for the server. But this is a difficult hit to keep in-bounds, and such a crosscourt shot must be long and high, giving right-front and right-back time to reach it.

COMMUNICATION

If your team has any hopes of playing strategic volleyball, team members must communicate with each other while the ball is in play.

Like outfielders in baseball, volleyball players have overlapping jurisdictions on the court. Balls are often hit into those gray areas, challenging two or more teammates to decide who should take it. Sometimes beginners fall back on a *Bad News Bears* kind of defense: banging into each other on one play, then backing off and letting the ball fall between them untouched on the next one.

Talk to each other to prevent this. A back-row player usually takes on the quarterback role, loudly calling out who should take the ball hit to the gray area. This allows the backs to focus on passing and frees the fronts to move forward for the attack. On any ball they are sure they can take, back-row players should loudly call out "Mine!" or "Me!" Agree as a team on one call so everyone knows what to listen for.

If the opponent's hit is near a boundary line, the players going after the ball may not know if the ball is in or out; they must rely on teammates to guide them. If the ball is clearly going to land out-of-bounds, the call is "Out!" or "No!" If the ball appears to be in-bounds, on the line, or too close to let drop, call "Good!" or "Yes!"

In intermediate play, blocking and spiking are an integral part of the game. Advanced players expect a spike and block on almost every play. Thus, when the ball loops over the net, eliminating the need for a block, the call is "Free!"

Even intermediate volleyball teams want their designated setter to make the second touch; to accomplish this, the setter may have to go a ways to reach errant passes. When it becomes clear to the setter that she cannot reach the ball for the second hit, she should cry "Help!"

SPECIALIZATION

Beginning volleyballers should not specialize; that is, no one person should play designated spiker or setter all the time.

Instead, middle-front should automatically set, and left-front and right-front should attack. In this way, novices get to practice every skill. As you improve, you will inevitably become better at some facets of the game than others. Specialization then allows you to reinforce your strengths or work on your weaknesses.

SPIKE VERSUS TIP

Like a fastball pitcher with a change-up, a spiker will be more effective if he also has a tip. Because a soft tip is easy to return if the opponents can reach it, you need to direct it to open court. Rather than hit it high over the blocker's outstretched hands, tap it just high enough to evade the blocker.

Play a tip early in the game. That tells the opponents it's part of your arsenal and makes them wonder when they'll see it again. Don't use the tip too often, or you'll lose the element of surprise.

WINNING
THE MENTAL GAME

You are bound to master the physical skills of volleyball long before the mental ones. When you get hooked on a new sport, you appropriately tend to concentrate exclusively on the muscular activities. Only after developing some shots and moves can you begin to play the mental game. That is, in volleyball first you learn to pass-set-smash, then you learn to "think."

And make no mistake, volleyball is a thinking game. Even as a recreational hacker, mastering the so-called inner game of volleyball can give you a competitive advantage. If you mentally fortify yourself with the techniques in this chapter, you can become a better player. Strive for the three Cs: concentration, consistency, and confidence.

CONCENTRATION

If you talk to accomplished athletes in any sport, you will hear them speak of the importance of concentration. Sometimes called focus, it's at the heart of success in any endeavor, including volleyball.

Most everyone knows that concentration has to do with paying attention. Does that mean consciously willing yourself to focus? Is concentration a shrill voice in your head screaming over and over, "Pay attention!" until you do? Maybe at first.

Focus is delicate, elusive. Pay close attention to the trees and you may miss the forest, and vice versa. Eventually, if you stay with it, you will learn to relax and focus more naturally. Once you master the techniques and know when to use them, you may be able to turn game control over to your now well-developed instincts.

Your conscious mind, however, will want to interfere. Consider this athletic equation:

Performance = Potential – Interference

Performance is how well you actually do—your results; potential is a measurement of the best performance you are capable of at any given moment; interference is the mental static produced by the conscious mind. When pressure is minimal, the mind may become distracted: "Wonder where Michelle is right now. . . . How about those Cowboys! . . . Boy, do I look stunning in this tank top!"

As pressure mounts, so do self-doubts and anxiety, two other prime causes of mental static. Again, the conscious mind rushes in, usually to provide a litany of advice: "Deep breaths . . . eye on the ball . . . elbow up . . . hand to the ear . . . snap the wrist . . . whoops!"

With all that advice raining down on you, is it any wonder that you're tighter than last year's pants?

And what happens when you're tight? The unwanted contraction of only a few extra muscle fibers in the arms is enough to cost you power and timing, turning a handsome spike into a net burner.

Returning to our equation, it's clear that a reduction of mental interference will improve performance, even with no change in potential (read: practice). In other words, get your head screwed on right and you can become a better player without even picking up a ball.

But the overactive conscious mind does not react well to being told to butt out. (It's rather like ordering yourself to sleep.) Instead, you will have to rely on deceit. Some coaches suggest distracting the conscious mind by focusing on something only marginally related to the task at hand. By having something else to chew on, the subconscious is left unfettered.

Here are some ways to distract that pesky conscious mind.

Associate Positively. Suppose you are serving for the match. Like everyone, you've had both good and bad moments in the past. For best results, zero in on the successes and ignore the failures. Replay an imaginary tape that you might call "My Greatest Hits." Immerse yourself in positive recollections.

Visualize. First cousin to positive association, visualization is a type of mental rehearsal in which you conjure up detailed visions of the activity before you do it.

The first step is to relax, using a method that works for you. You might close your eyes and take a few deep breaths, recite your favorite mantra, or play a mental videotape of a winning moment. You may see it from your own perspective or through the eyes of an omniscient being, whichever is more comfortable.

Focus on the finer points of, say, the hit. Immerse yourself in it. See it as one fluid whole. Hear the muted thump of the ball against your skin; feel its leathery roundness, its heft; see your fingers guiding the ball; see the ball zipping toward its target.

The power of visualization received a lot of publicity in the seventies with the revelations of several famous athletes. Golfer Jack Nicklaus said that he never hit a shot without first seeing the ball's perfect flight followed by its "sitting up there high and white and pretty on the green." A successful shot, according to Nicklaus, was 50 percent visualization, 40 percent setup, and only 10 percent swing.

Visualization takes dedicated practice, but you can do it anywhere—in bed or in a bathtub, at a bus stop—and the rewards are significant. I have interviewed and profiled more than forty world-class athletes, most of whom attribute some, if not most, of their success to visualization.

Research suggests that your muscles respond to visualization of an act almost as if you did the act. Thus, the more intensely you visualize the perfect spike, the more entrenched it will become in your muscle memory. This kind of memory operates almost entirely on the subconscious level, which helps explain how you can make a great play but can't explain it to others.

Swing by the Numbers. Count to three each time you serve, spike, or pass. Either silently or aloud, count "one" at the end of the backswing, "two" at contact, and "three" on the follow-through. Try to synchronize the sound of your voice with the act. It's harder than you think, and the conscious mind should be fully

Here are some tips for winning the mental game:

1. Two minutes before a match, do sixty seconds of stomach breathing. At the changing of sides in a match, a few seconds of stomach breathing keeps the brain alert, even though the body is tired.
2. Always have a complete ten-minute warm-up before a match, even if you have to do it off the court.
3. Given the choice of sides at the start of a match, always choose the worst side first. (The quality of the sides is usually governed by background or lighting. The wind may also be a factor outdoors.) It is better to finish the match on the best side of the court (although if there is a third game, a coin flip will decide that). In the first game, before either team has acclimatized, it is less of a disadvantage to have the worst side.
4. Play your normal game in the first instance against an unknown opponent. But if it's not successful, be ready to try something different.
5. If your opponents are on a winning streak, don't let them rush you. If they try, do what you can to slow the pace. Use your time-outs accordingly.
6. Plain water or glucose drink is the only thing to drink during a match, and it should be limited to a few mouthfuls. Instead, hydrate before and after the match.
7. Remember that there is no such thing as a complete player or team. Your opponents are only human, despite the doubts you harbor during slumps. They have weaknesses and can be beaten.

engaged trying to accomplish it. Try it during practice and see if it works for you. You may find that counting—"one, two, three . . . one, two, three"—lends to your hitting motion a rhythm it lacked.

Study the Opponent. Spend time before a match limbering up both physically and mentally. Whether your opponents are strangers, acquaintances, or friends, get into the habit of studying them and their play. Besides such obvious matters as whether they are left- or right-handed or walk with a limp, study the subtleties. Routinely ask yourself the following questions:

- What are their weaknesses? Strengths? Favorite moves?
- How is their net play? Are they more likely to spike or tip?
- Who's the setter? Spiker?
- Can others set? Spike?
- How do they handle balls hit right at them?
- What are their serving tendencies? Do they telegraph them?
- Do they display different mannerisms when tired?

Smart players make adjustments that help them succeed. For example, if your opponents begin shaking out their arms or displaying other signs of fatigue, quicken the pace and try to move them quickly around the court. If opponents reveal an early weakness, exploit it. Find the weak serve-returner with your serves.

ATTITUDE

The biggest difference between the competent and the excellent in any sport is mental preparation. Successful athletes find a way to remain, or quickly regain, calm. To be effective, you must keep a check on counterproductive emotions. Some of us play better than others when we're mad; no one plays well in a rage. Analyze missed hits, but don't dwell on them.

PRESSURE

As you improve and play better competition, the pressure mounts. It is often pressure that causes a great player to blow a pass he's made thousands of times before.

Picture this scenario: You're behind in a match against a pretty good local team in your neighborhood or club. You have to win your serve to stay in the game. There are a few people watching, and you feel the rivalry. Your guts are twisting like wet

> "**I** was going to buy a copy of *The Power of Positive Thinking,* but then I thought: What the hell good would that do?
>
> —Ronnie Shakes

rope—*that's* pressure. Most everyone feels it at one time or another. The real question is, can you control it? Successful people don't dodge pressure; they make it work to their benefit.

Others seem to be able to block pressure out entirely. Orlando Magic center Jon Koncak denied that having to replace injured Shaquille O'Neal put pressure on him: "Pressure to me is being in an airplane and the pilot dies and they ask me to fly the plane."

GETTING BETTER

....

The key to becoming a better volleyball player is to practice, practice, practice—you heard it here first. Your practice sessions should have a purpose—perhaps to improve a certain skill—and be as gamelike as possible. Besides playing a lot of volleyball, try the following drills to combine specific skills.

TWO-SKILL COMBINATION DRILLS

Once you have learned at least two skills, you can link them, as you would in a real game. The following drills will help you do that.

Simulated Serve and Pass. You need three players and two balls for this drill. A tosser (simulated server) stands at the attack line on one side of the net; on the other side, midway between the attack line and the baseline, stands a receiver, with a target person near the net and to the right (fig. 17).

The tosser uses two hands to throw the ball over the net toward the receiver, who calls for the ball and bumps it to the target person. Meanwhile, the target has delivered a second ball to the tosser, who immediately puts it in play with another two-hand toss. A quick, continuous pace makes the drill aerobic and allows instincts full reign. Try for eight successful forearm passes out of ten, each of which moves the target person no more than a step.

Serve and Bump for Accuracy. Three players and one ball are in nearly the same arrangement as for the last drill. This time, however, the tosser becomes a legitimate server, using an underhand style from behind the baseline (fig. 18). The receiver/passer should focus on both height and accuracy, bumping the ball well above the net and within one step of the target person. Rotate positions after ten serves.

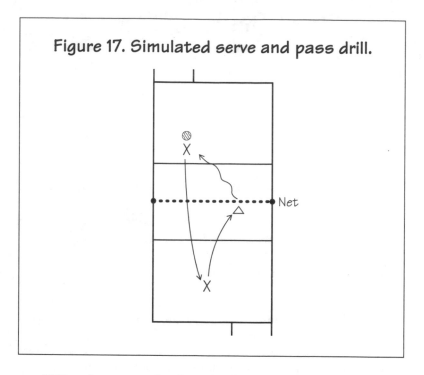

Figure 17. Simulated serve and pass drill.

With only two people, the passer can aim for a 10-foot-square target that can be moved around the court. The disadvantage is that someone has to retrieve the passes and return them to the server.

Calling for the Serve. Two receivers stand at the left-back and right-back positions, with a server on the opposite side. A target or target person is positioned near the net.

The server hits a variety of serves to the backcourt, moving the ball around to all three deep positions. One of the receivers calls for each serve and passes it to the target, as in previous drills. Try for six successful forearm passes out of ten.

THREE-SKILL COMBINATION DRILLS

The ultimate goal of a beginning team striving to become an intermediate team is to master the three-hit sequence of bump, set, and attack. The following drills combine those skills with a serve.

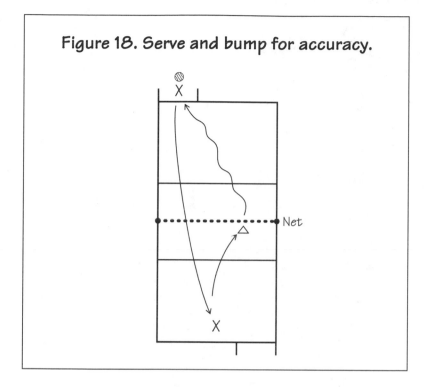

Figure 18. Serve and bump for accuracy.

Serve, Bump, and Set. With four players, put a server in one service area and a passer, setter, and attacker on the other side. Start with the passer in the left backcourt, the setter at the right net, and the target person just outside the left sideline (fig. 19).

The server makes an underhand serve to the passer, who bumps to the setter. The setter, who should not have to move more than a step in any direction, sets the ball high and outside, aiming at least 6 feet higher than the net and no more than a foot from the left sideline. The target person lets the ball bounce to check its accuracy, then returns the ball to the server. Rotate and work on all skills.

Serve, Bump, and Back-Set. This drill is the same as the previous one, except that the receiver takes the serve in the right-back, and the setter back-sets the ball well above the net to within a foot of the right sideline.

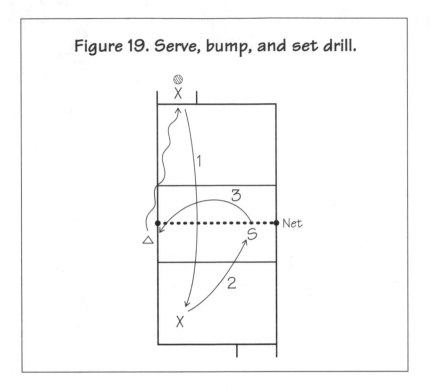

Figure 19. Serve, bump, and set drill.

Reception Decision. With five players, put a server on one side and four players on the other side. Two receivers occupy the backcourt, a setter is right front, and a target person is outside the left sideline.

The ball is served underhand to center backcourt. The receivers react to the ball and someone calls for it, ideally before it reaches the net. The ball is bumped to the setter who, as always, should not have to move more than a step. The setter sets the ball high and outside, at least 6 feet higher than the net and within a foot of the left sideline. The target person lets it bounce to gauge its accuracy, then returns it to the server.

As you rotate through the three hitting positions, keep track of your results to compare your relative strengths.

Serve, Pass, and Set. Two teams of four players each compete against each other in this drill. Each team has its server on

Figure 20. Serve, pass, and set game drill.

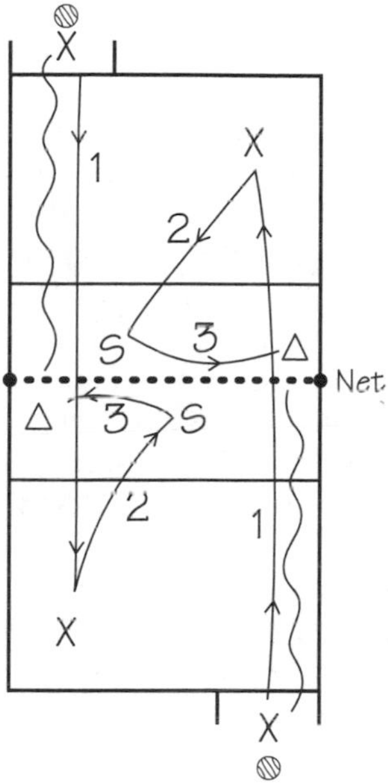

one side of the net and its forearm passer, setter, and target person on the other side, directly across from the server (fig. 20).

Both teams serve at the same time. Score one point each time a team completes the combination of legal serve, good bump, and good set. As always in these drills, a good bump is one hit to within a step of the setter. A good set is a ball that arcs at least 6 feet higher than the net and lands within a foot of the left sideline. The target person lets the set bounce and returns it to the serving teammate on the opposite side.

Pass, Set, and Spike. The tosser throws the ball hard over the net deep into the opposite backcourt, where the passer directs it to the setter with a forearm bump. The setter sets the ball high and outside for the attacker, who spikes the ball over the net.

Time the rotations to allow players to work on the weak parts of their game.

FOUR-SKILL COMBINATION DRILLS

To be successful, your team must be able to receive your opponents' serve, cushion its impact, and then seamlessly switch from defense to offense. If you are unable to handle this transition, you will be forced to return a free ball to your opponents. Hit in a manner other than an attack, a free ball is easy to handle, and it gives opponents the opportunity to regain the advantage with a smooth transition to offense.

Here are some drills to grease the transition wheels.

Serve, Bump, Set, and Attack. You need four players: a server on one side and a passer, setter, and attacker on the other (fig. 21). The serve goes underhand from the service area to the receiver in first one deep corner and then the other. The receiver passes to the setter, who tries to set the ball at least 6 feet above the net and within 1 foot of the sideline. The attacker hits the ball over the net using a variety of weapons, from tip to spike. Try to get the four-part sequence right at least half the time.

> "Show me a thoroughly satisfied man—and I will show you a failure."
> —Thomas Edison

Serve, Bump, Back-Set, and Attack. This drill is the same as the previous one, except that the setter back-sets over his head to the attacker.

Continuous Three-on-Three. Teams of three players each line up one behind the other off the baseline of one side of the court. Each team has a volleyball. Another team begins on the opposite side (the winner's court) without a ball.

The first team in line serves and runs out onto the court. If the receiving team returns the ball with the proper three-touch sequence—pass, set, and attack, no tips allowed—the rally continues until play is over. After the initial return of serve, the ball may be returned in less than three hits, although that should not be encouraged.

Figure 21. Serve, bump, set, and attack drill.

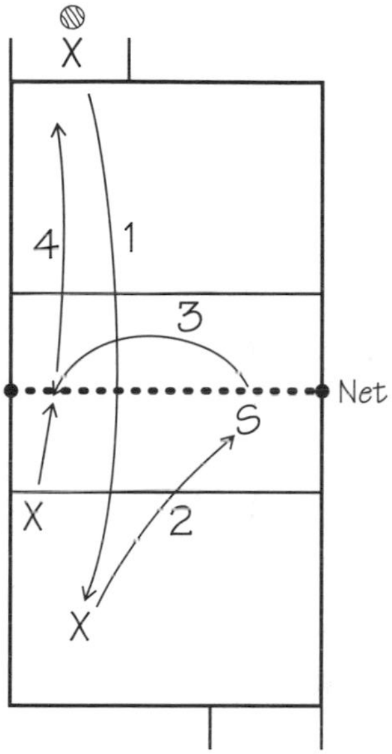

The winning team scores a point and gets to play in the winner's court; the losing team goes to the end of the line. The goal is to make it to the winner's court and hold it as long as possible.

Attack Line Tip. Two teams of three players play a game with the attack lines as end lines, shortening the court and effectively eliminating spikes (fig. 22). The serve-receiving team must execute the proper three-hit combo. Play continues until one team wins the rally and the point. The losing team then puts the ball in play with an overhead toss. Play to an agreed-upon number of points.

One-Third Court Game. Two teams of two players each compete, using a court with normal length but only one-third normal width (fig. 23).

Play begins with a serve from the baseline and continues until an error is made. Score two points for each three-hit combination and one point for each winning rally.

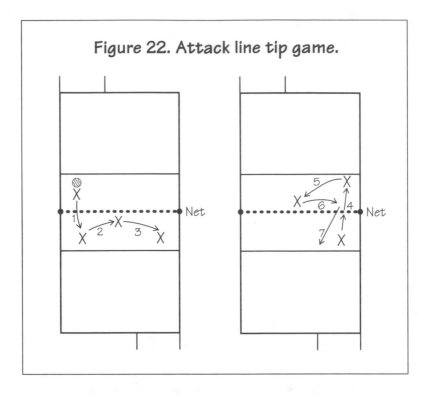

Figure 22. Attack line tip game.

John Kessel, program director for USA Volleyball, believes in providing specific feedback to players. Here's his Top 10 list of nonspecific feedback:

10. That's it.
 9. Keep that up.
 8. Way to go.
 7. That's okay.
 6. Don't do that.
 5. I like that.
 4. Good job.
 3. Nice try.
 2. That's not it.
 1. (Silence with a quizzical look)

Figure 23. One-third court game.

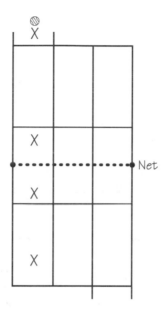

Net

Even less helpful, he believes, is negative, nonspecific feedback:

10. Don't worry.
9. Don't serve into the net.
8. Don't set it so close.
7. Don't push me.
6. Don't question me.
5. Don't be stupid.
4. Don't do that.
3. Don't net.
2. Don't give up.
1. Don't, just don't.

SOLO PRACTICE

Volleyball is a good game to play with friends. But sometimes, like Charlie Brown standing alone on the pitcher's mound in a downpour, you want to play and no one else is around. If so, there are drills you can do by yourself.

Try to play with a net or reasonable facsimile. If you have no net, use a clothesline, or draw a line on the ground and play with an imaginary net. "The more you use a net," says John Kessel, "the better you will become."

Serve against the Wall. Mark a line on a wall the same height as the top of the net. Stand back 30 feet or more and serve

John Kessel's twenty coaching sound bites that will actually improve play.

20. Don't compare, become
19. Relentless pursuit
18. Talk is cheap
17. Winning and losing are temporary, friendships last forever
16. Every dog has its day
15. It's not where you are, it's who you are
14. There is no such thing as try
13. Everything changes
12. Practice hard, play ferociously
11. The power of modeling is awesome
10. Random learning makes us better players
9. Program over team, team over individual
8. Motivation through competition
7. Be innovative, not imitative
6. Have FUN—it is a game
5. Make it gamelike
4. Coach for understanding
3. Quality over quantity
2. Create what you need
1. There is no magic

over that line. Make sure your serves clear the net, because a serve that even brushes the net is side-out. As you go through your routine, visualize powerful, accurate serves.

Serve and Dash. A full serve includes a sprint to the back row, so add that to your routine. As you move onto the court, watch the ball and note any changes you should make in the next serve.

Pass into a Corner. With a wall in front of you and a corner to your right, throw a ball off the wall so it rebounds back as if it were being served to you. Move to the ball, absorb the blow, and pass it into the corner, as if to a setter. Retrieve the ball and do it again.

Dig to Yourself. Throw the ball off the wall so that it comes back to you in different positions, especially low ones. Work on digging every ball you can touch, trying to direct it straight up, then move under it and make a good set. In general, it's best to dig up (to teammates), not over (to opponents).

Spike against the Wall. Stand at least 30 feet from a wall, set the ball to yourself, and spike it over the net line. You won't be able to get into the same kind of rhythm you can when someone else is setting for you, but you can try to perfect an arm swing. Set the ball both low and high and hit crosscourt and line shots.

Juggle. Like a soccer or hacky sack player, dribble the ball off your head, thighs, and knees to gain agility. (Using the lower body has been legal worldwide since 1995.) See how many times in a row you can hit the ball without its falling to the floor.

RULES

....

U.S. Outdoor Volleyball Rulebook
(abridged version)

These rules are endorsed by the California Beach Volleyball Association, the Women's Professional Volleyball Association (WPVA), Midwest Volleyball Professionals (MVP), and the following national tours: Spike-It-Up, Bud Light U.S. Pro-Am, and Jose Cuervo. With a few exceptions, they are the rules that govern both indoor and outdoor play.

For the complete Official Outdoor Volleyball Rules, contact USA Volleyball Publications at 800/275-8782. Proceeds from the sale of the rule book benefit the U.S. National, Olympic, and Junior Olympic Beach Volleyball teams.

1. Playing Area

1.1 Dimensions. The playing area consists of a rectangular playing court measuring 59' by 29'6" and a surrounding free zone that is a minimum of 9'10" wide.

1.2 Playing Surface. The surface of the playing area must be as flat and uniform as possible, free of rocks, sprinkler heads, and any other objects that may cause injury. Sand courts consist of fine-grained sand and should be at least 12" deep. Grass courts consist of maintained grass surfaces free of holes, puddles, and uneven ground. Any hazardous areas should be designated as out of play.

1.3 Lines on the Court. Boundary lines consist of two sidelines and two endlines, which mark the playing court. They are made of $1/4$" to $3/8$" rope or $1/8$"-wide flat bands or tape. The centerline divides the playing court into two square team courts, but is [usually] not marked. Attack lines are marked 9'10" from the centerline (net). All lines are considered to extend indefinitely.

It is the players' responsibility to assure that all lines are in their proper location prior to the start of each play. Lines moved during play do not cause the rally to stop. If it cannot be determined whether a ball lands in bounds or out of bounds, it is a replay.

1.4 **Service Zone.** The service zone is behind the endline and between the extension of the sidelines and extends to the end of the free zone.

2. Net and Posts

2.1 **Height of the Net.** The height of the net is 7' 11$^{5}/_{8}$" for men and 7' 4$^{1}/_{8}$" for women, measured at the center. A net failure occurs when there is a sudden loss of net height or tension. If the net failure is the result of a fault or does not affect the outcome of the rally, the rally counts. Otherwise, it is replayed.

3. Ball

3.1 **Ball.** The ball must be spherical, made of flexible leather or water-resistant leatherlike cover and a rubber or rubberlike bladder. Its circumference must be 25$^{1}/_{2}$"–26$^{1}/_{2}$" and its weight 9–10 ounces. It may be of any color or multicolored.

4. Teams

4.1 **Composition.**
Doubles: 2 players on the court per team, no more than 2 on the roster.
Triples: 3 players on the court per team, no more than 3 on the roster.
Four-person: 4 players on the court per team, no more than 6 on the roster.
Six-person: 6 players on the court per team, no more than 12 on the roster.
All competitions must involve teams with the required number of players. Teams with fewer than the required number of players must forfeit.

Mixed teams are composed of male and female players competing on a men's height net; Reverse Mixed teams compete on a women's-height net. Mixed teams must contain equal numbers of males and females on each team, except in triples (where there must be at least one of each) or if otherwise specified.

Females may compete in men's tournaments, but may not play the male role in any other type of competition. Males may not play the female role in any type of competition.

4.2 Captain. The captain is the one player who represents his or her team in dealings with the officials. In doubles, both players have the rights of the captain.

5. Players' Equipment

5.1 Equipment. A player's clothing must be presentable and appropriate for the competition. Players on the same team are permitted to wear clothing of different colors and designs. Players may wear hats, visors, or sunglasses at their own risk. Players may play barefoot, in socks, or in booties. Shoes may be worn, but they cannot have any type of nonflexible cleats or spikes.

5.2 Forbidden Objects. It is forbidden to wear any objects that may cause an injury to a player, such as jewelry, pins, bracelets, casts, etc. Players may wear glasses or flat-band rings at their own risk.

6. Rights and Responsibilities

6.1 Players. All participants must know the official USA Volleyball Outdoor Rules and abide by them.

Participants must behave respectfully and courteously in the spirit of fair play toward the refereeing corps, teammates, opponents, and spectators. They must refrain from actions aimed at delaying the game or taking unfair advantage.

Participants must accept referees' decisions with sportsmanlike conduct. In case of doubt, clarification may be requested. A captain may protest the referee's interpretation of a rule, but not the referee's judgment.

7. Scoring System

7.1 To Win a Match. Matches may either consist of a single game, or best two out of three games. A team wins a match by winning one or two games, respectively.

7.2 To Win a Game.

(a) One game match: 15 points, win by 2, no cap (limit).

(b) First or second game in 2 out of 3: 11 points, win by 2, no cap.

(c) Deciding game in 2 out of 3: 7 points, win by 1, 7–6 wins.

7.3 To Win a Rally. Whenever a team fails to serve or return the ball, or commits any other fault, the opposing team wins the rally.

If the serving team wins a rally, it scores a point and continues to serve. If the receiving team wins a rally, it gains the right to serve, but does not score a point (side-out).

7.4 Default and Incomplete Team. A team declared incomplete for the game or match loses the game or match. The opposing team is given the points.

8. Preparation of the Match

8.1 Coin Toss. Before the warm-up in the first game and before each deciding game, the first referee conducts a coin toss in the presence of the team captains. The winner of the coin toss chooses either: (a) to serve or receive service of the first ball, or (b) the side of the court on which to start the game.

The loser takes the remaining alternative and, for the second game in a 2 out of 3 match, gets to select from the above choices.

9. Team Lineup

9.1 Rotation Order. The rotation order specified by the starting lineup must be maintained throughout the game. (There is an exception for doubles.)

9.2 Substitutions. (2 or 3 players) No substitutions or replacements of players are allowed.

(4 or 6 players) Unlimited substitutions are allowed as long

as one player does not occupy more than one position in the service order during a single game. Abnormal substitutions may be allowed in case of injury.

10. Positions

10.1 Players' Positions at the Time of Service.
(2, 3, or 4 players) Players may be anywhere within their court.

(6 players) Same overlap rules as indoor play. All players, except the server, shall be within the team's playing area. They may be in contact with the boundary lines or center-line, but may not have any part of their body touching the floor outside those lines.

All players shall be in correct serving order. The center front shall not have a foot touching the floor as near the right sideline as the right front nor as near the left sideline as the left front. The center back shall not have a foot touching the floor as near the left sideline as the left back. The center back on the receiving team shall not have a foot touching the floor as near the right sideline as the right back. No back-row player shall have a foot touching the floor as near the centerline as the corresponding front-row player.

After the ball is contacted for the serve, players may move from their respective positions.

11. States of Play

11.1 Ball in Play. The ball is in play from the service contact until the ball is out of play.

11.2 Ball Out of Play. The ball is out of play from the moment the ball lands or a fault is committed. The rally ends when a referee halts play or the ball is out of play.

11.3 Ball in Bounds. A ball is in when its first contact with the ground is on the playing court or a boundary line.

11.4 Ball Out of Bounds. The ball is out when:
(a) Its first contact with the ground is completely outside the playing court, and it does not cause boundary lines to move;

(b) It completely crosses the net outside the posts or under the net after the attacking team's third contact;

(c) It touches an object out of play.

12. Playing Faults

12.1 Definition. Any playing action contrary to the playing rules is a fault. If two or more faults are committed successively, only the first one is counted, except when the first fault is the ball contacting the ground and the second fault occurs during the continuation of the play. If two or more faults are committed by two opponents simultaneously, the rally is replayed.

13. Playing the Ball

13.1 Team Contacts. Each team is entitled to a maximum of three contacts to return the ball to the opponents. A player may not contact the ball two times consecutively except during or after blocking or at the team's first contact. Blocking does not constitute a team contact, and any player may make the first contact of the ball after the block.

13.2 Simultaneous Contacts. If two opponents simultaneously and instantaneously contact the ball over the net, the ball remains in play and the team receiving the ball is entitled to another three hits. If such a ball lands out of bounds, it is the fault of the team on the opposite side of the net from where the ball lands.

(2 or 3 players) A joust occurs when players of opposing teams cause the ball to come to rest above the net through simultaneous contact. A joust is not a fault, and play continues as if the contact was instantaneous.

13.3 Assisted Hit. A player is not permitted to take support from a teammate or any object in order to reach the ball. However, a player who is about to commit a fault may be stopped or held back by a teammate.

13.4 Characteristics of Contact. A player may touch the ball with any part of the body. A player may have successive contacts with the ball during a single attempt to make the team's first contact with the ball, provided that the fingers are not used to direct the ball. The ball must be contacted cleanly and not held (including lifted, pushed, caught, carried, or thrown). The ball cannot roll or come to rest on any part of a player's body.

(2 or 3 players) An exception is allowed during the defensive play of a hard-driven ball, which is an attack-hit or blocked ball traveling at a high rate of speed (as judged by the referee). In that case, the ball may be momentarily lifted or pushed, providing that the attempt is one continuous motion and the player does not change the direction of the motion while contacting the ball. A contact of the ball with two hands, using the fingers to direct the ball, is a set. A player may set the ball in any direction toward his/her team's court, provided that the ball is contacted simultaneously by both hands and does not visibly come to rest.

Rotation of the ball after the set may indicate a held ball or multiple contacts during the set, but in itself is not a fault. A legal set directed toward a teammate that unintentionally crosses the net is not a fault, regardless of the player's body position. Intent is judged by the referee.

(2 or 3 players) If the ball is intentionally set into the opponent's court, the player must contact the ball above his/her shoulders and must direct the ball perpendicular to the direction his/her shoulders are facing.

(2, 3, or 4 players) When contacting the ball with one hand, it must be cleanly hit with the heel or palm of the hand (a roll shot), with straight, locked fingertips (a cobra), knurled fingers (a camel toe), or the back of the hand from the wrist to the knuckles. One-handed placement or redirection of the ball with the fingers (a dink or open-hand tip) is a fault.

14. Ball at the Net

14.1 Ball Crossing the Net. A ball directed to the opponents' court must go over the net within the crossing space, limited as follows:

- Bottom is bounded by the top of the net;

- Sides bounded by the posts and their imaginary extensions;
- Top bounded by any structure or obstacle, including the ceiling.

14.2 Ball Touching the Net. The ball may touch the net while crossing the net, except during the service. A serve that touches the net is a fault.

14.3 Ball in the Net. A ball driven into the net may be recovered within the limits of the team's three touches.

15. Player at the Net

15.1 Reaching beyond the Net. While blocking, players may touch the ball beyond the net, provided they do not interfere with the opponent's play, before or during the attack-hit.

A player is permitted to pass his/her hands beyond the net after an attack-hit, provided that the contact was made within his/her team's playing space.

Within the limits of the three-team contacts, a player may contact a ball that has crossed the net below the net, or outside the posts, in an attempt to recover a ball that has not been contacted by the opponents. The recovered ball must cross the centerline below the net or outside the posts.

15.2 Penetration into Opponent's Playing Area. Players may partially or completely cross the centerline below the net or outside the poles, either before, after, or during a legal play of the ball, provided that this does not interfere with the opponent's play. Incidental contact with an opponent is ignored, unless such contact interferes with the opponent's opportunity to play the ball. While opposing players are not required to avoid the ball or the player, they cannot intentionally interfere with any legal attempt to play the ball on their court.

If a player crosses the centerline and interferes with an opponent during the continuation of a play, it is a fault.

15.3 Contact with the Net or Posts. It is a fault for a player or a player's clothing to touch any part of the net. Exceptions:

- Incidental contact of the net by a player's hair;

- A player's hat, visor, or glasses fall off during play and then contact the net;
- A ball is driven into the net, or the wind blows the net, causing it to touch a player.

Once a player has contacted the ball, the player may touch the posts, ropes, or any other object outside the total length of the net, provided that it does not interfere with play.

16. Service

16.1 Definition. The service (or serve) is the act of putting the ball into play by the serving player in the service zone.

16.2 Service Order. If the serving team wins the rally or a replay is directed, the player who served the previous rally serves again. If the serving team loses the rally, the next server on the receiving team serves the ball.

(2 players) If a player is discovered serving out of order, that player continues to serve with no loss of points. The opposing team remains in its serving order, but the offending team will reverse its original order of service to ensure that no player will serve three consecutive terms. Excessive misuse of this privilege is unsportsmanlike conduct.

16.3 Authorization of Service. It is the responsibility of the server to assure that both teams are ready for service. A player on the receiving team may stop play when not ready for a service, as long as no attempt to play the ball is made. In this case, the rally is canceled and replayed. Misuse of this privilege is unsportsmanlike conduct.

16.4 Execution of Service. The server may move freely behind the endline. At the moment of service or take-off for service, the server must not touch the ground outside the service zone. The player's foot may not go over a boundary line. After the service contact, the player may land on the court or outside the service zone.

The server contacts the ball with one hand or any part of the arm after clearly tossing or releasing the ball and before the ball touches the playing surface.

16.5 Service Attempt. If the server releases the ball for service but does not attempt to complete the service motion, the referee will cancel the rally and direct a replay. A player may only receive one such replay during any one term of service.

16.6 Screening. The server's teammates must not prevent the opponents, through screening, from seeing the server or the path of the ball. On an opponent's request, a player must move sideways, bend over, or bend down.

17. Attack-Hit

17.1 Definition. All actions to direct the ball toward the opponent's playing area, except in the act of serving and blocking, are considered to be attack-hits. An attack-hit is completed the moment the ball completely crosses the vertical plane of the net or is touched by a blocker. A player may contact an attack-hit at any height, provided that contact with the ball is made within the player's own playing space.

    (back-row player on 6-person tream or male on Reverse Mixed team) If a player contacts the ball completely above the height of the net and the player's foot is touching or has last touched the ground on or in front of the attack line, the attack-hit must have an upward trajectory.

17.2 Attack-Hit Faults. It is a fault when a player completes an attack-hit on the opponent's service, if the ball is entirely above the height of the net.

18. Block

18.1 Definition. Blocking is the action of a player(s) close to the net to deflect the ball coming from the opponent by reaching above the height of the net.

18.2 Hits by the Blocker. The first hit after the block may be executed by any player, including the player who touched the ball at the block.

18.3 Block within the Opponent's Space. In blocking, the player may place his hands and arms beyond the net, provided that action does not interfere with the opponent's play. The player is not permitted to touch the ball beyond the net until the opponent has made an attack-hit.

18.4 Blocking Contact. A blocking contact is not counted as a team hit. The blocking team will have three hits after a blocking contact. Consecutive, quick, and continuous contacts may occur by one or more blockers, provided that these contacts are made during one blocking action.

(2, 3, or 4 players) There are no restrictions on which players may participate in a block.

(6 players) Back-row players may not participate in a block.

(Reverse Mixed teams) Male players may not participate in a block.

When a ball is blocked back into an attacking player, the attacker is not considered to be a blocker. Therefore, that contact counts as the first of the team's three hits.

19. Time-Outs

19.1 Definition. A time-out is a regular game interruption. It lasts for 30 seconds. Each team is entitled to a maximum of four time-outs per game. Successive time-outs may be requested without resumption of the game.

20. Delays to the Game

20.1 Definition. A delay is an improper action of a team that defers resumption of the game and includes:
- Prolonged time-outs, after being instructed to resume the game;
- Repeating an improper request in the same game;
- Delaying the game;
- (4 or 6 players) Delaying a substitution.

20.2 Sanctions for Delays. The first delay by a team in a game is sanctioned with a delay warning. The second and any subsequent delay of any type by the same team in the same game constitutes a fault and is sanctioned with a delay penalty, which is the loss of a rally.

21. Exceptional Game Interruptions

21.1 Injury. If an injury occurs as the result of a fault or does not affect the outcome of the rally, the rally counts. Otherwise, the rally is immediately canceled and replayed.

When no legal or abnormal substitute is available, an injured player is given a five-minute injury time-out. This will not be granted more than twice for the same player in one game.

21.2 External Interference. If external interference does not affect the outcome of play, the rally counts. Otherwise, the rally is immediately canceled and replayed. A shouted warning, such as "Ball on!" is sufficient to affect the outcome of play, provided that a player had a chance to make a legal play of the ball. Misuse of this privilege is unsportsmanlike conduct.

22. Court Switches

22.1 Court Switches. Court switches are team exchanges of playing courts, which occur at specified times during a game:

- 15-point games, when the total number of points is a multiple of five;
- 11-point games, when the total number of points is a multiple of four;
- 7-point game, when the total number of points is a multiple of two.

23. Misconduct

23.1 Categories. Incorrect conduct by a team member toward officials, opponents, teammates, or spectators is classified in four categories according to the degree of the offense:

- Unsportsmanlike conduct: arguing, intimidating, taking unfair or inappropriate advantage of player privileges, etc.
- Rude conduct: acting contrary to good manners or moral principles, interfering with an opponent's ability to play,

expressing contempt.

- Offensive conduct: defamatory or insulting words or gestures.
- Aggression: physical attack or intended aggression.

23.2 Sanctions. Depending on the degree of the incorrect conduct, according to the judgment of the first referee, the sanctions to be applied are:

- Misconduct warning: For unsportsmanlike conduct, no penalty is given, but the team member concerned is warned against repetition in the same game.
- Misconduct penalty: For rude conduct, the team is penalized with the loss of one rally.
- Expulsion: Repeated rude conduct is sanctioned by expulsion. The player must leave the playing area for the remainder of the game.
- Disqualification: For offensive conduct and aggression, the player is sanctioned by disqualification and must leave the playing area for the remainder of the match. Disqualified players may be subject to further sanctions by the Tournament Director.

23.3 Sanction Scale. Repetition of misconduct by the same person in the same game is sanctioned progressively. Disqualification due to offensive conduct or aggression does not require a previous sanction.

23.4 Misconduct before and between Games. Any misconduct occurring before or between games is sanctioned and the sanction(s) apply in the following game.

24. Refereeing Corps and Procedures

24.1 Procedures. Hand signals are used to start a rally and voice commands are used in all other situations. When used, whistles halt play, authorize service, or accept or deny a request.

The first referee authorizes service by giving the signal for service, and halts play to end a rally when he/she is sure that a fault has been committed and has identified its nature.

25. First Referee

25.1 Authority. The first referee directs the match from start to finish. The first referee has authority over the refereeing corps and the team members. During the match the first referee's decisions are final. The first referee is authorized to overrule the decisions of other members of the refereeing corps and may replace any member who is not performing assigned duties properly.

The first referee has the power to decide any matter involving the game, including those not provided for in the rules.

The first referee does not permit any discussion about game decisions. However, at the request of a captain, the first referee may explain the application or interpretation of the rules on which the decision was based. A captain, having immediately indicated disagreement with the explanation, reserves the right to submit an official protest of the incident at the end of the match. The first referee must authorize this.

GLOSSARY

ace: A serve that scores a point without any opponent's touching the ball.

antennae (aerials): The rods that protrude above the top of the net and define the width of the attacking area. All balls must be hit across the net between the antennae without touching them. The ball is out-of-bounds if it touches or crosses the net outside of the antennae.

attack: To smash the ball into the opponents' court.

attacking block: A block aimed at putting the ball straight down into the attacker's court.

attack line: A line on the court 9.5 feet (3 meters) away from, and parallel to, the net. (See also *frontcourt*.)

attack system: The method of attack a team uses to try to beat the opponents' blocks.

audible: A play called in midralley.

auxiliary setter: The player, usually right-front, designated to set when the primary setter cannot.

backcourt: The area of the court between the attack line and the baseline.

backcourt spike: A spike by a backcourt player.

back set: A set made over the setter's head to a player behind her.

back-row player: A player who starts the rally from behind the attack line. In six-person volleyball, it is any player who assumes positions 1, 5, or 6.

back slide: A quick slide behind the setter.

baseline: A line parallel to the net and 29.5 feet (9 meters) from it.

block: To jump in the air and intercept or divert a ball from the opponents' court, using the hands, arms, or upper part of the body. A player who makes a block may touch the ball a second successive time without penalty. The block and subsequent touch count only as one hit.

block cover: Players not participating in the block who cover any ball hit past the block.

blocker: A player who takes part in a block.

break: An abrupt change of direction in the attacker's approach.

break point: The spot where the attackers change direction.

centerline: The imaginary line beneath the net that divides the court in two.

combination play: An offensive strike involving two or more attack players acting in concert.

court: The playing area including the boundary lines but not including the service area.

cover: To protect any area of the court to which the ball may travel. Backcourt players should try to *cover the hitter,* that is, back up their own hitters whose blocks may rebound to an unguarded part of the court.

crosscourt attack: A smash hit at a steep angle across court.

dead ball: A ball no longer in play.

deep: Away from the net and toward the baseline.

deep set: A ball set or passed well away from the net.

defensive player: Any player of a team not in possession of the ball.

dig: To play the ball below the waist, with one or two hands.

double-block: A block executed by two players.

double-foul: Two simultaneous fouls by players of opposing sides.

double-hit: A foul in which the same player touches the ball twice in succession. A ball hit again by the blocker after her block is legal and not considered a double-hit.

dump: A surprise tip by the setter, usually on the second team touch. It can catch the opponents off guard, especially if the dumper camouflages her intentions, making it look like a routine set.

fake smash: A play in which an attacking team pretends to smash, but then dumps, volleys, or sets the ball.

floater: A serve that darts in an unpredictable path.

follow-through: The movement of the arm after the ball has been contacted.

foot fault: The penalty incurred when the server's foot touches the playing surface, including the baseline, before contacting the ball, or any other player's foot touches the opposing court.

formation: The alignment of players in attack or defense.

free ball: A slow, arcing shot

that the receiving team is "free" to attack as it likes.

frontcourt: The area between the attack line and the net. Only frontcourt players can spike from inside this area.

front-row players: The three players nearest the net, whose official court positions are 2, 3, and 4.

game plan: A team's offensive and defensive strategy for a particular opponent, including starting rotation.

held ball: A foul in which the ball seems to be caught or comes to rest momentarily on any part of a player's body.

inside: Toward the center of the net—that is, away from the sidelines.

jump serve: A serve in which the player jumps and attacks the ball, as in spiking.

jump set: A set made by a frontcourt player while she is in the air.

kill: A hard shot angled downward that the opposing side is unable to return.

kinesthesia: The sensation of movement, position, and tension of parts of the body. All other things being equal, greater kinesthetic awareness will make you a better player.

lineup: A team's serving order, which reflects the players' starting locations on the court.

load: To arrange the blockers so that the best ones confront the opponents' best attackers.

lob pass: A ball passed in a high arc.

match: A predetermined number of games, or sets. In major indoor events, a match usually consists of best of five sets; local matches tend to be best of three sets.

multiple attack: An offensive play executed by two or more players.

multiple block: A block executed by two or more players.

multiple contact: Touching the ball more than once on the same play. This is allowed as long as no two contacts are made by the same player in succession (other than by a blocker after the block).

net ball: A ball that touches the net, except on the service (see *net serve*). If a net ball continues across into the opponents' court, the ball is alive and in play.

net fault: An illegal act whereby a player touches the net while the ball is in play. It is not a fault if the contact was caused by the ball's forcing the net into the player's hand or body, or if it was accidentally caused by a player not playing the ball.

net serve: A serve that hits the net; it is a fault even if the ball continues across into the opponents' court.

offense: The team playing the ball.

out-of-bounds: The area beyond the outside edge of the boundary lines. The ball is also out-of-bounds if it hits the antennae or crosses the net outside of the antennae.

outside: Away from the center of the court and toward one sideline or the other.

overlap: A foul in which one player is out of position relative to a teammate when the ball is served.

overset: A ball that is accidentally set across the net.

pancake: A technique in which a player flattens his hand against the floor in order to save the ball.

pass: To deliver the ball from one player to another without its touching the floor or any obstruction.

penetration: Movement of a backcourt player to the net to act as a setter, leaving the three frontcourt players to act as spikers.

pepper: A warm-up drill in which two players pass, set, and hit the ball back and forth.

positioning: Location of the players in the lineup. They must hold the same positions until there is a change of server on their own team.

post: The standard that supports the net.

quick serve: To start service as soon as possible after the referee has blown for the service to be made. If the receiving team is slow to react, the serving team may gain an advantage.

quick (short) set: A low set for an incoming spiker made possible by an accurate first pass.

quick smash: A spike of a quick set or directly from the first pass.

rally: The period from the serve to the end of play.

recovery: The act of diving to successfully retrieve a hard-hit or cleverly placed shot.

rotation: To advance one position clockwise in the lineup. Rotation takes place only when a team gains or regains the serve.

roundhouse: Type of attack shot played with the arm fully extended above the head.

scoop: A fault in which a player lifts the ball with open hands.

screen: An illegal act by the players of the serving team, who position themselves to block the opponents' view of the server.

seam: The midpoint between two players.

service area: The area behind the baseline from which the server puts the ball in play.

set: (1) A high pass, designed to enable a teammate to spike; (2) a volleyball game, usually played to fifteen points.

shallow: Near the net.

shank: A severely misdirected forearm pass.

side-out: Change of service that occurs when the serving side loses a rally. Service ends and passes to the opponent.

simultaneous contact: Contact made at the same time by two players.

spike (smash): To hit the ball forcefully into the opponents' court. Front-row players can spike from anywhere on the court; back-row players must begin their jump from behind the attack line when spiking.

stuff: To block the ball to the floor.

substitution: The means by which players may be replaced by other players once the ball is dead. Six substitutions per side are allowed in each set. A substitute may be substituted for in the same set, but, except for injury, only by the player he replaced in the first place.

switch: To move around the court and assume positions best suited to the individuals' play. This is legal if done after the service.

tape: The top of the net.

telegraph: To give away one's intentions to the opponents.

time-out: A pause during a set when the players may rest or confer with a coach. Two time-outs are allowed per team per set. Each lasts a maximum of thirty seconds and may be called only when the ball is dead.

tip: A soft, arcing hit that drops close to the net.

transition: The change from defense to offense, or vice versa.

volley: The basic skill of passing the ball forward or backward using two hands.

warm-up: The preparatory exercises each team does before a match.

RESORCES

··

Three governing bodies currently oversee volleyball competitions in the United States. All collegiate women's play and some scholastic girls' competitions are governed by the rules of the National Association for Girls and Women in Sport (NAGWS). Contact NAGWS at 1900 Association Dr., Reston, VA 22091.

Boys' high school play and most girls' high school play is governed by the National Federation of State High School Associations (NFSHSA), at 11724 Plaza Circle, Box 20626, Kansas City, MO 64195.

Men's and women's open, men's collegiate, and almost everyone else use rules handed down by USA Volleyball (USAV). Founded in 1928 as the United States Volleyball Association, USAV is the national governing body for the sport and the parent organization of the USA men's and women's national teams.

USAV seeks to nurture all variations of the game—indoor, grass, sand, six-person, doubles, coed—at all skill and age levels. Besides supporting a year-round training schedule for the Olympic teams, USAV oversees USA Youth Volleyball (ages 7–12), the Junior Olympic Volleyball program (ages 12–18), the U.S. Open Championships, and the USA Coaching Accreditation Program (CAP). USAV also establishes rules of play in the United States and certifies referees and scorekeepers.

For administrative purposes, USAV divides the country into regions. You can contact the national office in Colorado to find out who your commissioner is. All commissioners have information about registration, player eligibility, and tournament schedules. You can order books and videos directly by calling 1-800-275-USVB.

For rule information and interpretation:
USA Volleyball
3595 E. Fountain Blvd.
Colorado Springs, CO 80910-1740
Tel 719-637-8300; Fax 719-597-6307

John Kessel, the Director of Program Development for USA Volleyball, is responsible for developing programs below the national team level. Contact him at the above address or by E-mail at jkessel@usa-volleyball.org. His World Wide Web site is http://www.volleyball.org/usav/jkessel.html.

On the international level, the Federation Internationale de Volley Ball (FIVB) was founded in 1947 in Paris for the expressed purpose of organizing and promoting the sport around the world. The FIVB currently has member associations in 210 countries, which are grouped into five continental confederations. USA Volleyball is a member of the Norceca Confederation.

Disabled Volleyball

Founded in 1967 by disabled Vietnam veterans, Disabled Sports USA offers sports and recreation programs to people with physical disabilities. Contact them at 451 Hungerford Drive, Suite 100, Rockville, MD 20850; tel 301-217-0960; fax 301-217-0968.

The organization also sponsors the U.S. Disabled Volleyball Team (USDVT), made up of players who are "standing physically disabled athletes." According to Disabled Sports USA Executive Director Kirk Bauer, "It is the first disabled volleyball team in history to compete head-to-head with able-bodied teams."

In addition, the USDVT represents the United States at international disabled sports competitions, including the Paralympic Games, the Olympic-level competition held quadrennially for athletes with physical disabilities. The team finished fourth at the 1992 Paralympics in Barcelona.

The Name Game

Perhaps you need a name for your volleyball team. If, on the one hand, you want to keep it light and unintimidating, either because you want to lull the opponents into thinking you're terrible or because you really are terrible, here are some suggestions:

Scared Hitless
Hit for Brains
Hit-eating Grinners
Doesn't Mean Hits
Blockheads
Balls Out
By the Balls
Balls in an Uproar
The Sandeaters
The Blazing Sunburns
The Bumping Maniacs
Heads in the Sand
We Could Carry Less
Spiked Punch
Vertically Challenged
Death at the Net
Lost Boys
Straight Down
Bump Uglies
Court Jesters
Folly for Serve

If, on the other hand, you want to strike fear into your opponents' hearts, consider the following:

Serves You Right
Set to Kill
Spin Doctors
Death at the Net
Sand Blasters
Over the Top
Diggin' and Swingin'
Arm and Hammer
Mass Spikes
Sand Storm

Super competitive types who have lost all perspective will prefer these titles:

In Your Face
Duck or Bleed
This Won't Take Long
Wanted For Malicious Kills

Statistics

Volleyball may not lend itself to statistical analysis the way baseball does, but it's not without its symbols, averages, and percentages. To wit:

Kills Average	K/G = Kills/Games Played
Attack Percentage	PCT = Kills-Errors/Attempts
Total Attempts	TA = Kills + Errors + O Hits
Assists Average	ASG/G = Number of Assists/Games Played
Assists Percentage	PCT = Assists/Assist Attempts
Ace Average	A/G = Number of Aces/Games Played
Dig Average	D/G = Number of Digs/Games Played
Block Average	
Individual	B/G = BS + BA/Games Played
Team	B/G = BS + ½ BA/Games Played